50 Activities for Teaching Emotional Intelligence

The Best From Innerchoice Publishing

Level I: Elementary

Introduction and Theory
by
Dianne Schilling

Innerchoice Publishing, Torrance, California 90505

Cover Design: Doug Armstrong Graphic Design

Illustrations: Roger Johnson, Zoe Wentz, and Dianne Schilling

ISBN: 1-56499-032-X

INNERCHOICE PUBLISHING
P.O. BOX 1185
TORRANCE, CALIFORNIA 90505
Tel. (310) 816-3085 Fax (310) 816-3092

Over the last decade or so "wars" have been proclaimed, in turn, on teen pregnancy dropping out, drugs, and most recently violence. The trouble with such campaigns, though, is that they come too late, after the targeted problem has reached epidemic proportions and taken firm root in the lives of the young. They are crisis intervention, the equivalent of solving a problem by sending an ambulance to the rescue rather than giving an inoculation that would ward off the disease in the first place. Instead of more such "wars," what we need is to follow the logic of prevention, offering our children the skills for facing life that will increase their chances of avoiding any and all of these fates.

—Daniel Goleman

Contents

Contents

Contents

How to Use . . .
50 Activities for Teaching Emotional Intelligence

Inspiration and Origins

This activity guide is a collection of the most popular and effective emotional literacy activities offered by Innerchoice Publishing over the past ten years. The activities have been compiled expressly for the purpose of helping you apply the theory and recommendations of authorities in the field of brain-based education and emotional learning, including behavioral scientist and best-selling author Daniel Goleman (*Emotional Intelligence: Why It Can Matter More Than IQ*).

Like many educators, Goleman views "the curriculum" as a plan for ongoing comprehensive age-appropriate lessons taught school wide. Based on this definition, he is correct in concluding that very few schools currently have an emotional intelligence curriculum. Goleman asserts, "In theory, there is no reason why such a curriculum could not be taught in every school nationwide. It already exists in many, but only in bits and pieces...not as a fully developed, step-by-step curriculum."

Over the years, Innerchoice Publishing has contributed hundreds of "bits," "pieces" and fully-developed programs to thousands of schools throughout the country. You are invited to use this newest contribution to the EQ curricular mosaic as:

- the core of your emotional literacy curriculum

- a specialized EQ supplement to your existing curriculum

The bottom line is, don't neglect or take for granted the emotional life of your students. Feelings, self-awareness, life skills, conflict management, self-esteem, and all of the other developmental areas now identified as affecting emotional intelligence are critically important. An impressive array of brain-based research supports the validity of time and energy spent by educators in these domains. Emotions are not unruly remnants of stone-age survival to be hushed and otherwise ignored while we develop cognitive skills. Emotions drive our behavior, shape our values, and predispose us to choose one course of action over others. Emotional and rational skills are equally important interdependent components of human intelligence.

Unit Organization

The ten units in this guide each contain five activities, and comprise a complete emotional literacy curriculum. They are:

• *Self-awareness*

Knowing the likes, dislikes, hopes, preferences, cultural heritage, talents, shortcomings, and other uniquenesses that make up the individual. Becoming aware of inner and outer states and processes.

• *Managing Feelings*

Building a vocabulary for feelings; knowing the relationship between thoughts, feelings and actions; accurately reading feeling cues in others and responding appropriately; realizing what is behind feelings (e.g. the primary feelings underlying anger) and learning how to constructively express and control feelings.

• **Decision Making**

Examining what goes into making decisions; learning a step-by-step process for decision making; applying the process to real issues.

• **Managing Stress**

Understanding what stress is, where it comes from, and how it affects daily living; learning to use exercise, diet, guided imagery, relaxation methods, and attitude changes to control and relieve stress.

• **Personal Responsibility**

Examining actions and knowing their consequences; learning when and how to say no; recognizing the existence of personal choice in almost all situations; taking responsibility for decisions and actions.

• **Self-concept**

Establishing a firm sense of identity and feeling esteem and acceptance of oneself; monitoring "self-talk" to catch negative messages such as internal put-downs; acknowledging the talents and abilities of self and others.

• **Empathy**

Taking the perspective and understanding the feelings of others; developing caring and compassionate attitudes.

• **Communications**

Learning and practicing effective communication skills; using I-statements instead of blame; listening actively.

• **Group Dynamics**

Working self-reflectively in groups while monitoring behaviors and roles; practicing cooperation and interdependence; knowing when and how to lead and when to follow.

• **Conflict Resolution**

Understanding that conflict is normal and potentially productive; learning how to fight fair with others; learning and practicing a variety of conflict-resolution strategies, including win-win approaches to negotiating, compromise, and problem-solving.

Each of the ten units contains three group activities and two fully developed Sharing Circles, along with a list of additional Sharing Circle topics, which allow you to repeat the impact of the powerful circle process for many weeks. Before you lead your first Sharing Circle, be sure to read the section, "EQ Super Strategy: The Sharing Circle" beginning on page 19.

Many of the activities include handouts, called "Experience Sheets," for you to duplicate and distribute to students. Experience sheets are written in a conversational style and speak directly to the individual student. Directions for their use are imbedded in the printed procedure for leading each activity.

The units are arranged in a suggested order, but may be implemented with considerable flexibility. We encourage you to maintain an agile, expansive attitude as you move through (or skip among) the units. Allow the reactions of students to spark new ideas for strengthening emotional literacy skills in each topic area.

Finally, please make any adjustments necessary to accommodate the interests, abilities, cultural backgrounds and learning styles of your students. Your experience and regular contact with students put you in an ideal position to interpret signals regarding relevancy and modify the activities accordingly.

Schooling the Emotional Mind

Children have two minds — one that thinks and one that feels. An inch or so beneath the curls, buzz jobs and baseball caps, just behind the contact lenses and lashes, sit two systems operating two different yet interdependent intelligences: rational (IQ) and emotional (EQ). How children function each day and throughout life is determined by both. Rational intelligence cannot perform well without emotional intelligence, and emotional intelligence benefits from the cool cognitive judgments of the rational mind. When the two perform together smoothly and efficiently, emotional intelligence rises and so does intellectual ability.

Thanks to psychologist and author Daniel Goleman, the term *Emotional Intelligence* has become part of our daily lexicon. Goleman's best-seller *Emotional Intelligence: Why It Can Matter More Than IQ* , a superb presentation of research from education, medicine, and the behavioral and brain sciences, forms the basis for much of the ensuing discussion as well as the accompanying strategies and activities.

What Is Emotional Intelligence?

The American Heritage Dictionary defines emotion as "an intense mental state that arises subjectively rather than through conscious effort and is often accompanied by physiological changes" and as "the part of the consciousness that involves feeling; sensibility."

The word *emotion* is a derivative of the Latin root, *movere*, to move. Anyone who has experienced intense joy, desire, anger, or grief knows that emotions are anything but static mental states. Emotions are something we *do*.

Emotions shift our attention and propel us into action, rapidly organizing the responses of different biological systems — facial expression, muscle tone, voice, nerves, hormones — and putting us in optimum condition to respond. Emotions serve to establish our position relative to our environment, pulling us toward certain people, objects, actions, and ideas, and pushing us away from others. They allow us to defend ourselves in dangerous situations, fall in love, protect the things we value, mourn significant loss, and overcome difficult obstacles in the pursuit of goals.

The words *emotion* and *motivation* are closely related. In order to be strongly motivated we have to *feel* strongly. We are moved to *do* things, and we are moved *by* things. In Goleman's words, "Every strong emotion has at its root an impulse to action; managing those impulses is basic to emotional intelligence."

The terms *emotional intelligence, emotional literacy, emotional competence,* and *emotional competencies* are used in varying contexts throughout these pages. *Emotional intelligence* is the <u>capacity </u>to acquire and apply information of an emotional nature, to feel and to respond emotionally. This capacity resides in the emotional brain/mind. *Emotional literacy* and *emotional competence* are used interchangeably to describe the relative <u>ability </u>to experience and productively manage emotions. The shorthand for these terms is EQ. *Emotional competencies* are <u>skills </u>and <u>attributes </u>— self-awareness, empathy, impulse control, listening, decision making, anger management — whose level of development determines the strength of our emotional intelligence and the degree of our emotional competence.

The Sentry and the Strategist

Experts and explorers in the field of brain-based education have known or suspected for many years that emotions are the ignition switch and the octane for learning. Curriculum developers in the self-esteem arena (including this publisher) have been developing emotional intelligence under the guise of self-esteem and life-skills education for at least two decades. However, not until Goleman's book have we seen such a startling configuration of scientific evidence — case after case demonstrating the power of the emotional mind to override rational intelligence for both good and bad consequences.

The Sentry

A small structure in the limbic region of the brain, the *amygdala*, is the center of the emotional mind. All incoming data to the brain pass through the amygdala where they are instantly analyzed for their emotional value before going to the cerebral cortex for processing. Data leaving the amygdala carry an emotional charge, which, if sufficiently powerful, can override reasoned thinking and logic.

The amygdala is the specialist in emotional matters, the storehouse of emotional memory, and the seat of passion. The amygdala allows us to recognize the *personal significance* of daily events, which in turn provoke pleasure, stir compassion, arouse excitement, and incite rage.

The amygdala plays the role of sentry, scanning every incident for signs of trouble. Far quicker than the rational mind, it charges into action without regard for the consequences.

In an emotional emergency, the amygdala proclaims a crisis, recruiting the rest of the brain to its urgent agenda. Goleman calls this an *emotional hijacking*, because it occurs instantaneously, moments before the thinking brain has had a chance to grasp what is occurring and decide on the best coarse of action.

Emptying the mailbox at the end of her driveway, Marci senses a blur of movement across the street and looks up to see an elderly woman stumbling to the ground. A man is sprinting down the sidewalk with something dangling from his hand. Mail scattering in her wake, Marci flies across the street and after the man, screaming "Drop it," "Drop it." A purse bounces from the sidewalk to the gutter. Marci sees it but continues running, finally slowing to a jog as the snatcher disappears over a fence.

This is an example of an emotional hijacking. What Marci did wasn't rational. She neither witnessed a crime nor checked with the assumed victim; she didn't even see the purse until it hit the ground. Marci's emotional mind spliced together a few visual cues and produced a small feat of heroism which she had no opportunity to evaluate until it was over. What Marci felt as she jogged back to sooth her elderly neighbor, was an abating storm of outrage. Marci's own purse had been stolen a few months earlier.

In moments of crisis or intense passion, such as Marci's, the habits of the emotional brain dominate, for better or for worse. That is why, after an emotional hijacking, we express surprise at our own behavior. "I probably shouldn't have done that. I don't know what came over me," was Marci's rational evaluation moments after she returned the purse and reflected on her behavior.

The warp speed responses of the emotional mind take place without entering conscious awareness. Their purpose is to protect us from danger — to keep us alive. Our earliest ancestors needed these split-second reactions in situations where decisions had to be made instantly. Run or fight. Hide or attack. Actions that spring from the emotional mind have been measured at a few thousandths of a second and carry an overwhelming sense of certainty.

The Strategist

The critical networks on which emotion and feeling rely include not only the limbic system (amygdala), but also the neocortex — specifically the prefrontal lobes, just behind the forehead. This part of the emotional brain is able to *control* feelings in order to reappraise situations and deal with them more effectively. It functions like the control room for planning and organizing actions toward a goal. When an emotion triggers, within moments the prefrontal lobes analyze possible actions and choose the best alternative.

In the wake of intense fear or anger, for example, the neocortex is capable of producing a calmer, more appropriate response. It can even muffle emergency signals sent out by the amygdala. However, this mechanism is slower, involving more circuitry.

In Marci's case, control came too late. It isn't that she threw caution to the winds. Her own safety did not become a consideration until after the chase was over.

Internal Battles

So far, the amygdala and neocortex sound like perfect partners, the alert sentry signaling danger and the cool strategist selecting prudent courses of action. But the sentry can easily overreact, and powerful emotions can disrupt our ability to think and reason. Fear can render us mute or maniacal; anger can make us lash out visciously.

In such moments, the circuits from the amygdala to the prefrontal lobes are creating neural static, sabotaging the ability of the prefrontal lobe to maintain working memory. That's why we complain that we "can't think straight" when we are upset.

These emotional circuits, and the automatic reactions they convey, are sculpted by experience throughout childhood. Emotionally-driven automatic responses are usually learned very early — as early as four years of age. According to Goleman, all it takes is for some feature of the present situation to resemble a situation from the past. The instant that feature is recognized by the emotional mind, the feelings that went with the past event are triggered. *The emotional mind reacts to the present as if it were the past.* The reaction is fast and automatic, but not necessarily accurate or appropriate to the situation at hand. Frequently we don't even realize what is happening. Goleman describes it like this:

The emotional mind uses associative logic. It takes elements that symbolize reality or trigger a memory of it to be the same as reality. While the rational mind makes logical connections between causes and effects, the emotional mind connects things that have similar, striking features. The rational mind reasons with objective evidence; the emotional mind takes its beliefs to be absolutely true and discounts evidence to the contrary. That's why it's futile to try to reason with someone who is emotionally upset. Reasoning is out of place and carries no weight. Feelings are self-justifying.

The Impact of Emotional Intelligence

Emotions impact every area of life: health, learning, behavior, and relationships.

Children and young people who are emotionally competent— who manage their own feelings well, and who recognize and respond effectively to the feelings of others — are at an advantage in every area of life, whether family and peer relationships, school, sports, or community and organizational pursuits. Children with well-developed emotional skills are also more likely to lead happy and productive lives, and to master the habits of mind that will assure them personal and career success as adults.

In homes and schools where emotional intelligence is nurtured with the same concern as IQ, children tolerate frustration better, get into fewer fights, and engage in less self-destructive behavior. They are healthier, less lonely, less impulsive, and more focused. Human relationships improve, and so does academic achievement.

Health

There is no longer any question that emotions can profoundly affect health. Science used to believe that the brain and nervous system were separate and distinct from the immune system. In fact, the two systems are in close communication, sending messages back and forth continuously. Furthermore, chemical messengers which operate in both the brain and the immune system are concentrated *most heavily* in neural areas that regulate emotion. Here are just a few of the implications:

- Inhibiting or constraining emotions compromises immune function. People who hide their feelings or refuse to talk about significant emotional upsets are at higher risk for a variety of health problems.

- Anger, and other negative emotions are toxic to the body and pose dangers comparable to smoking cigarettes.

- Studies have linked the colds and upper respiratory infections to emotional upsets that occurred three to four days prior to the onset of symptoms.

- Numerous studies have shown that positive, supportive relationships are good medicine, bolstering immune function, speeding recovery time, and prolonging life. The prognosis for people in ill health who have caring family and friends is dramatically better than for people without emotional support.

Learning

Almost all students who do poorly in school lack one or more elements of emotional intelligence. Study after study has shown that competence in emotional skills results not only in higher academic achievement on the part of students, but in significantly more instructional time on the part of teachers. Emotionally competent children are far less disruptive and require fewer disciplinary interventions.

Furthermore, academic intelligence, as measured by IQ and SAT scores, is not a reliable predictor of who will succeed in life. IQ contributes about 20 percent to factors that determine life success, which leaves 80 percent to other forces. Numerous studies have shown that IQ has minimal impact on how individuals lead their lives — how happy they are, and how successful. One major reason is that while cognitive skills are tied to IQ, desire and motivation are products of emotional intelligence. Children who are emotionally competent have an increased desire to learn and to achieve, both within school and without. Positive emotions — excitement, curiosity, pride — are the fuel that drives motivation. Passion moves young people toward their goals.

Behavior

Violence and disorder in America's schools have reached crisis proportions. Teachers who once dealt with mischievous, unruly students and an occasional temper tantrum are now demanding emergency phones in their classrooms, security guards in the hallways, and metal detectors at the gates. As long as such conditions continue, all education suffers. Rates of teen suicide, pregnancy, and drug abuse testify to the need for emotional literacy: self-awareness, decision-making, self-confidence, and stress management.

Relationships

Children who are effective in social interactions are capable of understanding their peers. They know how to interact with other children and adults — flexibly, skillfully, and responsibly — without sacrificing their own needs and integrity. They have a good sense of timing and are effective at being heard and getting help when they need it. Socially competent children can process the nonverbal as well as verbal messages of others, and recognize that the behaviors of one person can affect another. They take responsibility for their actions.

Children who cannot interpret or express emotions feel frustrated. They don't understand what's going on around them. They are frequently viewed as strange, and cause others to feel uncomfortable. Without social competence, children can easily misinterpret a look or statement and respond inappropriately, yet lack the ability to express their uncertainty or clarify the intentions and desires of others. They may lack empathy and be relatively unaware of how their behavior affects others.

Early Development

The first school for emotional literacy is the home. How parents treat their children has deep and lasting consequences for their emotional life.

In order to help children deal constructively with their emotions, parents must themselves have a reasonable degree of emotional literacy. The children of emotionally competent parents handle their own emotions better, are more adept at soothing themselves when they are upset, enjoy better physical health, are better liked by their peers, are more socially skilled, have fewer behavior problems, greater attention spans, and score higher on achievement tests.

Parents who ignore or show a lack of respect for their child's feelings, or who accept any emotional response as appropriate, are putting their child in peril not only for emotional development, but for intellectual development as well.

Bullies — children who tend toward violence — have parents who ignore them most of the time, show little interest in their lives, yet punish them severely for real or perceived transgressions. These parents are not necessarily mean-spirited, they are usually repeating parenting styles that were practiced on them in childhood. Intellectually, they may want the best for their children, but have no inkling how to achieve it.

The emotional skill that violent children lack above all others is empathy. They are unable to feel what their victim is feeling, to view the situation through the eyes of the other child. In many cases, this lack of empathy is due to parental abuse. Abuse kills empathy.

Children who are repeatedly abused often suffer from post-traumatic stress disorder (PTSD). When a child's life is in danger and there is nothing the child can do to escape the peril, the brain actually changes.

A structure within the brain of children with PTSD secrets extra-large doses of brain chemicals in response to situations that are reminders of traumatic events, even when present events hold little or no threat. Oversecretions also occur from the pituitary gland, which alerts the body to danger and stimulates the fight or flight response. Thus, PTSD is a *limbic disorder.*

The good news is that the behavior of emotionally troubled children — bullies and children with PTSD — can change. The emotional circuitry can be rewired through relearning.

Emotional Windows

Research indicates that being bold or shy, upbeat or melancholy is at least partially genetic. Children may be predisposed to a certain temperament based on the relative excitability of the amygdala. However these innate emotional patterns can be improved with the right experiences.

Early emotional learning poses a similar problem. Synaptic connections are formed very quickly, in a matter of hours or days. In Goleman's words, "Experience, particularly in childhood, sculpts the brain."

The key skills of emotional intelligence each have a critical learning period extending over several years in childhood. Massive sculpting of neural circuits takes place during these periods, each of which represents an optimal "emotional window" for learning specific skills. Once the emotional brain learns something, it never lets it go; once a window is closed, the pathway is forever etched. That's why changing in adulthood is so difficult. In fact, the patterns probably never change, though they can be controlled through new insights and with new learned responses.

The responses of the amygdala are well established long before a child leaves elementary school; however, the frontal lobes which regulate the limbic impulse mature into adolescence. Through skills and habits acquired at later ages, children can still learn to control their feelings, turn down the emotional thermostat, and substitute positive behaviors for negative.

Gender Differences

Girls receive significantly more education regarding emotions from their parents than do boys. In discussion, play, and fantasy, mothers cover a wider range of emotions with their daughters than with their sons.

Combine this greater knowledge with the fact that girls develop language skills more quickly than do boys and it is clear why girls find it easier to articulate their feelings and to use verbal exploration of feelings as substitutes for physical confrontations and fights, a difference that behavioral scientists have measured at about age 13. The chart summarizes gender differences in emotional intelligence.

Girls at 13:	Boys at 13:
• are adept at reading verbal and nonverbal emotional signals and expressing feelings.	• are adept at expressing anger
• experience a wide range of emotions with intensity and volatility.	• minimize emotions having to do with vulnerability, guilt, fear, and hurt.
• have learned to use tactics like ostracism, gossip, and indirect vendettas as substitutes for aggression.	• are confrontational when angry
• see themselves as part of a web of connectedness.	• take pride in a lone, tough-minded independence and autonomy

Controlling Emotions

If the sentry (the amygdala) and the neural pathways can't be changed, then the primary goal of emotional education is to improve the skills of the strategist — the neocortex. As we've seen, the neocortex is capable of managing the amygdala by reshaping its responses. Children will still have their emotional outbursts, but can learn to control how long they last and the behaviors they produce.

Psychotherapy is a classic example of this process, with the client engaging in systematic emotional relearning. Therapy teaches people to control their emotional responses. Consistent positive discipline — the kind that focuses on feelings underlying behavior and on identifying alternatives to unacceptable behavior — accomplishes the same thing.

The ability to bring out-of-control emotions back into line results in what our parents and grandparents called *emotional maturity.* Present terminology labels it *emotional competence*, the "master aptitude."

Self-Awareness

The first step in getting children to control their emotional responses is to help them develop self-awareness. Through self-awareness, children learn to give ongoing attention to their internal states, to know what they are feeling when they are feeling it, to identify the events that precipitate upsets and emotional hijackings, and to bring their feelings back under control. Goleman defines self-awareness as:

...awareness of a feeling or mood and our thoughts about the feeling. ...a slight stepping-back from experience, a parallel stream of consciousness that is "meta": hovering above or beside the main flow, aware of what is happening rather than being immersed and lost in it.

Self-awareness allows children to manage their feelings and to recover from bad moods more quickly. Children who are self-aware don't hide things from themselves. Labeling feelings makes them their own. They can talk about fear, frustration, excitement, and envy and they can understand and speculate concerning such feelings in others, too.

Lacking self-awareness, children may become engulfed by their feelings, lost in them, overwhelmed by them. Unawareness of what is going on in their inner and outer worlds sets the stage for lack of congruence between what they believe or feel and how they behave. Feelings of isolation ("I'm the only one who feels this way.") occur when children are unaware that others experience the same range of feelings that they do. Without self-awareness children never gain control over their lives. By default, their courses are plotted by others or by parts of themselves which they fail to recognize.

Self-awareness can take the form of nonjudgmental observation ("I'm feeling irritated.") or it can be accompanied by evaluative thoughts ("I shouldn't feel this way" or "Don't think about that.") Although in and of themselves, emotions are neither right nor wrong, good nor bad, these kinds of judgments are common and indicate that the neocortical circuits are monitoring the emotion. However, to try to abolish a feeling or attempt to take away a feeling in someone else only drives the emotion out of awareness, where its activity along neural pathways continues unmonitored and unabated — as neuroses, insomnia, ulcers, and communication failures of all kinds testify.

Managing Anger and Curbing Impulses

Eric started his day, not to the sounds of the birds or the local morning DJ, but to the jarring pre-dawn combat of his warring parents. The breakfast cereal was gone, the milk was sour, and there were no clean diapers for the baby whose fussing and screaming at length interrupted the din from the master bedroom. Accused of hurting the baby, Eric was scolded by his mother and slapped by his father. He fled the house without books or homework, almost missed the bus, and when he got to school was berated by his teacher for coming unprepared. At recess, Eric walked into the path of a speeding soccer ball, which stung his back and knocked him breathless. When he regained his wind, Eric found the boy who had kicked the ball and beat him until his face was bloody.

Eric had plenty of reasons to be angry. What he did not have, at least in this incident, were the internal skills or the external support system to help him process his feelings and prevent the anger from building.

Threats to life, security, and self-esteem trigger a two-part limbic surge: First, hormones called *catecholamines* are released, generating a rush of energy that lasts for minutes. Second, an adrenocortical arousal is created that can put a child on edge and keep him there for hours, sometimes days. This explains why children (including Eric) are more likely to erupt in anger over something relatively innocuous if the incident is preceded by an earlier upsetting experience. Though the two events may be completely unrelated, the anger generated by the second incident builds on the anger left over from the first. Irritation turns to anger, anger to rage, and rage erupts in violence.

Contrary to what many of us used to believe, when it comes to anger "letting it all out" is *not* helpful. Acting on anger will generally make a child angrier, and each angry outburst will prolong and deepen the distress.

What does work is to teach children to keep a lid on their feelings while they buy some time. If children wait until they have cooled down, they can confront the other person calmly. When flooded with negative emotions the ability to hear, think, and speak are severely impaired. Taking a "time out" can be enormously constructive. However 5 minutes is not enough; research suggests that people need at least 20 minutes to recover from intense physiological arousal.

Research has also shown quite conclusively that it's possible for a child to keep an angry mood going (and growing) just by thinking (and talking) about it.

> *Remembered or imagined experiences can create the same flood of chemistry as the experience itself*
> —Ellen Langer
> Harvard University, 1986

> *Thinking about a stressful situation produces the same bodily and mental responses as the experience itelf.*
> —American Medical Association
> Annual Research Conference, 1993

The longer a child dwells on what made her angry, the more reasons and self-justifications she can find for being angry. So when encouraging children to talk about their feelings, we need to be careful not to fan the flames.

Brooding fuels anger, but seeing things differently quells it. Reframing a situation is one of the most potent ways of controlling emotions.

Sadness: Shifting Gears

Depression and sadness are low-arousal states. When a child is sad, it's as though a master gauge has turned down everything: mouth, eyes, head, shoulders, speech, energy, motivation, desire. Taking a jog is probably the last thing the child feels like doing, but by forcing himself out the door and down the path, he will experience a lift.

The key seems to be shifting the mind from a low-arousal state to a high-arousal state. Exercise and positive distracting activities, like seeing a funny movie, turn up the master gauge, relieving sadness, melancholy, and mild depression. Another way to accomplish the shift is to engineer a small success, such as improving a skill, winning a game, or completing a project.

Humor is great at lifting children out of the doldrums and can add significantly to their creativity and ability to solve problems, too. In studies documenting the effects of humor, people were able to think more broadly, associate more freely, and generate more creative solutions and decisions after hearing a joke.

The ability of humor to boost creativity and improve decision making stems from the fact that memory is "state specific." When we're in a good mood, we come up with more positive solutions and decisions. When we're in a bad mood, the alternatives we generate reflect our negativity.

Choosing to watch cartoons, shoot baskets, ride a bike, or spend a few minutes on the computer is a decision that takes place in the neocortex. The amygdala can't be stopped from generating sadness and melancholy, but children can teach their neocortex a way out of the gloom.

Relationship Skills

If they are fortunate, children are surrounded by people who give them attention, are actively involved in their lives, and model healthy, responsible interpersonal behavior. Core skills in the art of relationships are empathy, listening, mastery of nonverbal cues, and the ability to manage the emotions of others — to make accurate interpretations, respond appropriately, work cooperatively, and resolve conflicts.

Howard Gardner's theory of multiplicity intelligence includes two personal intelligences, *interpersonal* and *intrapersonal*. People with high interpersonal intelligence have the capacity to discern and respond appropriately to the moods, temperaments, motivations, and desires of others. Intrapersonal intelligence gives people ready access to their own feeling life, the ability to discriminate among their emotions, and accurate awareness of their strengths and weaknesses.

The personal intelligences equip children to monitor their own expressions of emotion, attune to the ways others react, fine-tune their social performance to have the desired effect, express unspoken collective sentiments and guide groups toward goals. Personal intelligence is the basis of leadership.

Lacking personal intelligence, young people are apt to make poor choices related to such important decisions as who to befriend, emulate, date, and marry, what skills to develop and what career to pursue.

Components of Interpersonal Intelligence

- **Organizing groups:** directing, producing, leading activities and organizations

- **Negotiating solutions:** mediating, preventing and resolving conflicts, deal-making, arbitrating

- **Personal connections:** reading emotions and responding appropriately to the feelings and needs of others; teaming, cooperating

- **Social analysis:** insightful concerning the motives, concerns and feelings of others; able to size up situations

Components of Intrapersonal Intelligence

- **Self-knowledge and analysis:** having an accurate model of oneself and using that model to operate effectively in life; understanding own values, attitudes, habits, belief systems, strengths, weaknesses, and the motives that drive actions

- **Access to feelings:** the ability to discriminate among feelings and draw upon them to guide behavior; to identify and respond appropriately to own emotions

- **Personal organization:** the ability to clarify goals, plan, motivate, and follow through

- **Impulse control:** the ability to delay gratification; to deny impulse in the service of a goal

- **Fantasy and creativity:** the ability to nuture a rich and rewarding inner life

Empathy. All social skills are built on a base of emotional attunement, on the capacity for empathy. The ability to "walk in another's moccasins" is the foundation of caring and altruism. Violent people lack empathy.

Empathy is an outgrowth of self-awareness. The more we are able to understand our own emotions, the more skilled we are at understanding and responding to the emotions of others. Empathy plays heavily in making moral judgments. Sharing their pain, fear, or neglect is what moves us to help people in distress. Putting ourselves in the place of others motivates us to follow moral principles — to treat others the way we want to be treated.

These abilities have little to do with rational intelligence. Studies have shown that students with high levels of empathy are among the most popular, well adjusted, and high performing students, yet their IQs are no higher than those of students who are less skilled at reading nonverbal cues.

Empathy begins to develop very early in life. When infants and children under two witness the upset of another child, they react as if the distress were their own. Seeing another child cry is likely to bring them to tears and send them to a parent's arms.

From about the age of two on, when children begin to grasp the concept of their own separateness, they typically seek to console a distressed child by giving toys, petting, or hugging. In late childhood, they are able to view distress as an outgrowth of a person's condition or station in life. At this stage of development, children are capable of empathizing with entire groups such as the poor, the homeless, and victims of war.

Empathy can be developed through various forms of perspective-taking. In conflict situations, children can be asked to listen to each other's feelings and point of view, and then to feed back or summarize the opposing perspective. Imagining the feelings of characters in literature as well as figures from current events and history is also effective. Combining role playing with these strategies makes them even more powerful.

Nonverbal Communication Skills. The mode of communication used by the rational mind is words; the mode preferred by the emotional mind is nonverbal. We telegraph and receive excitement, happiness, sorrow, anger, and all the other emotions through facial expressions and body movements. When words contradict these nonverbal messages — "I'm fine," hissed through clenched teeth — nine times out of ten we can believe the nonverbal and discount the verbal.

Acting out various feelings teaches children to be more aware of nonverbal behavior, as does identifying feelings from videos, photos, and illustrations.

Emotions are contagious and transferrable. When two children interact, the more emotionally expressive of the pair readily transfers feelings to the more passive. Again, this transfer is accomplished *nonverbally.*

Children with high levels of emotional intelligence are able to attune to other children's (and adult's) moods and bring others under the sway of their own feelings, setting the emotional tone of an interaction.

Guided by cultural background, children learn certain display rules concerning the expression of emotions, such as minimizing or exaggerating particular feelings, or substituting one feeling for another, as when a child displays confidence while feeling confused. As educators in a multiethnic, multiracial society, we need to be sensitive to a variety of cultural display rules, and help students gain a similar awareness.

Listening. Through listening, children learn empathy, gather information, develop cooperative relationships, and build trust. Skillful listening is required for engaging in conversations and discussions, negotiating agreements, resolving conflicts and many other emotional and cognitive competencies.

Few skills have greater and more lasting value than listening. Unfortunately, listening skills are generally learned by happenstance, not by direct effort. The vast majority of children and adults are either unable or unwilling to listen attentively and at length to another person.

Research shows that poor listening impedes learning and destroys comprehension. However, when students are taught to listen effectively, both comprehension and academic performance go up, along with classroom cooperation and self-esteem. Listening facilitates both emotional learning and relearning — strengthening and refining the analytical and corrective functions of the neocortex.

Conflict Management. Schools are rife with opportunities for conflict. From the farthest reaches of the playground to the most remote corners of the classroom, from student restrooms to the teacher's lounge, a thousand little things each day create discord. The causes are many.

Children bring to school an accumulation of everything they've learned — all of their habits and all the beliefs they've developed about themselves, other people, and their world. Such diversity makes conflict inevitable. And because the conflict-resolution skills of most children are poorly developed, the outcomes of conflict are frequently negative — at times even destructive.

Diversity also breeds conflict. Learning to understand, respect and appreciate similarities and differences is one key to resolving conflicts. Unfortunately most of us learn as children that there is only one right answer. From the moment this fallacious notion receives acceptance, the mind closes and vision narrows.

Prejudice cannot be eliminated, but the emotional learning underlying prejudice can be *relearned*. One way to accomplish relearning is to engineer projects and activities in which diverse groups work together to obtain common goals. Social cliques, particularly hostile ones, intensify negative stereotypes. But when children work together as equals to attain a common goal — on committees, sports teams, performing groups — stereotypes break down.

Peer mediation programs offer another excellent avenue for relearning ineffective emotional responses to conflict. Mediators act as models, facilitators and coaches, helping their classmates develop listening, conflict resolution, and problem-solving skills.

Educating the Emotional Brain

Emotional intelligence is a core competence. To raise the level of social and emotional skills in students, schools need to focus on the emotional aspects of children's lives, which most currently ignore.

Unfortunately, in classes that stress subject-matter mastery, teaching is often devoid of emotional content. Too many educators believe that if somehow students master school subjects, they will be well prepared for life. Such a view suffers from a shallow and distorted understanding of how the human brain functions.

Joan Caulfield and Wayne Jennings, experts in brain-based education, specify four building blocks for incorporating emotional intelligence concepts in schools:

1. Safety, security, unconditional love and nurturing for every child

2. Stimulating classroom environments which provide rich sensory input to the brain

3. Experiential learning; opportunities to engage skills, knowledge and attitudes in a wide variety of real life tests

4. Useful and timely performance feedback

Many of the competencies that should be addressed by educational programs in emotional literacy have been specified on the previous pages. A number of outlines are suggested by Goleman in his book, *Emotional Intelligence*. One of the most useful comes from Peter Salovey, a Yale psychologist whose list of emotional competencies includes five domains and incorporates Howard Gardner's theories on interpersonal and intrapersonal intelligences.

1. **Knowing one's emotions:** Self awareness — recognizing a feeling as it happens. Monitoring feelings from moment to moment

2. **Managing emotions:** Emotional competence. Handling feelings; ability to recover quickly from upsets and distress;

3. **Motivating oneself:** Marshaling emotions in order to reach goals; self-control and self-discipline; delaying gratification and stifling impulsiveness

4. **Recognizing emotions in others:** Empathy — the ability to recognize, identify, and feel what another is feeling.

5. **Handling relationships:** The ability to manage emotions in others; social competence; leadership skills

To be most effective, emotional literacy content and processes should be applied consistently across the curriculum and at all grade levels. Children should be afforded many opportunities for skill practice, through a combination of dedicated activities and the countless unplanned "teachable moments" that occur daily. When emotional lessons are repeated over and over, they are reflected in strengthened neural pathways in the brain. They become positive habits that surface in times of stress.

Weaving EQ Into the Curriculum

Teachers may resist the idea of adding new content areas to the curriculum. In most cases, demands on teacher time are already at or beyond the saturation point, but this needn't be an insurmountable obstacle to emotional education. Feelings are part of everything that children do, and they can be part of everything they learn, too.

By incorporating lessons in emotional intelligence within traditional subject areas, we assist students to grasp the connections between realms of academic knowledge and life experience, and encourage them to utilize their multiple intelligences. This approach fits well with the concept of multidisciplinary teaching.

When a curriculum adheres to traditional straight and narrow subject areas and is devoid of emotional content, the subject matter is unlikely to "live" for students because of the curriculum's cold and reductionistic nature. With the world growing more complex by the minute, such an approach makes it extremely difficult for children to integrate the parts and pieces of what they learn, much less apply them within a real-world context.

By suggesting relationships and posing the right questions, by being observant and noticing nonverbal signals, teachers can help to surface and deal with emotional elements in every lesson, no matter what the subject area. Likewise they can take moments of personal crisis and turn them into lessons in emotional competence.

The Facilitator Role

Some teachers gravitate toward lessons in emotional intelligence and need little encouragement; if you are one of those, great! However, if you are uncomfortable talking about feelings, consider enlisting the help of the school counselor. Very little in traditional teacher education prepared you for this role, so start slowly and concentrate on becoming an effective facilitator of emotional inquiry. Here are just a few suggestions:

1. Rethink (and help colleagues, administrators, and parents rethink) traditional approaches to discipline. Substitute skill development for punishment, using misbehavior, upsets, and fighting as opportunities to teach children impulse control, conflict management, perspective taking, and awareness of feelings.

2. Strike a cooperative agreement with your school counselor. Invite the counselor to visit the classroom to lead emotional literacy activities.

3. Conduct class meetings to deal with issues and problems that the students submit for discussion. Create and decorate an "emotional mailbox" for the classroom, and encourage students to submit questions and problem descriptions.

4. Identify the dominant learning styles of individual students as a way of facilitating "flow." Flow is what we experience when we are so completely absorbed in a task or project that progress is effortless.

   In a state of flow, a child is completely relaxed yet intensely focused. Minimal mental energy is expended. Flow is characterized by an absence of limbic static and superfluous brain activity; emotions are positive and totally aligned with the task at hand.

An excellent way to encourage flow is to apply Gardner's theory of multiple intelligences, thus assuring that students engage in processes that are right for them and that utilize their competencies, learning styles, and talents. This allows the teacher to play to the strengths of children while attempting to shore up areas of weakness. As Goleman argues: "Pursuing flow through learning is a more humane, natural, and very likely more effective way to marshal emotions in the service of education."

5. Use cooperative learning principles and strategies. Cooperative learning optimizes the acquisition of subject-area knowledge while developing skills and concepts beyond those afforded by isolated study. Cooperation and collaboration mean that more information is discovered, processed, shared, and applied. And the fact that students process the information and find solutions along with their peers results in the development of a host of interpersonal and social skills.

By participating in team activities, students learn important lessons about group dynamics and develop extremely valuable communication skills. As students assimilate content, participating in team projects teaches them the value and skills of trust building, listening, respecting others' points of view, articulating ideas, planning, making choices, dividing the labor, encouraging others, taking responsibility, solving problems, compromising, managing and resolving conflicts, and celebrating team successes, to name just some of the benefits.

6. In addition to the emotional literacy activities in this book, be prepared for daily impromptu facilitation of emotional learning. For example:

• At a learning center, keep a doll-house replica of the classroom with a stick figure representing each student and the teacher. Allow the students to take turns pairing and teaming the figures to show who plays and works with whom, close friendships, antagonistic relationships, and where in the room individual students prefer to work. Use the same materials to reenact real conflicts that occur in the classroom.

• Order a video that shows a variety of emotions displayed via facial expressions or body movements. If a video is out of the question, collect photos from magazines. Have the students practice identifying the emotions from the nonverbal cues. Then invite them to act out the same emotions themselves.

• Work with children to bolster their sense of agency relative to the ups and downs in their lives. If a child shows signs of early depression, enlist the help of the school counselor. Children who are candidates for depression seem to believe that bad things (for example, a low grade) happen to them because of some inherent flaw ("I'm stupid"), and that there is nothing they can do to change these conditions. More optimistic children look for solutions, such as increased study time.

• Teach and counsel children to control anger in these ways:

—Change the thoughts that trigger anger, reassessing the situation with a different (less provocative) point of view. Often this involves looking at the situation from the other person's perspective. "Perhaps Sue is having a bad day." "Maybe Juan doesn't feel well." Changing thoughts produces new feelings which displace the anger.

—Cool off through active exercise or distracting activities.

—Write down angry thoughts and then challenge and reappraise them.

—Identify and express the feelings that precede anger. Anger is often a secondary emotion, erupting in the wake of other feelings, like frustration, fear, or humiliation.

—Monitor the feelings and bodily sensations they experience when they're becoming angry. Learn to use these sensations as cues to stop and consider what is happening and what to do about it.

Organizational EQ

Let's take a minute to talk about ourselves — our own emotional intelligence, and the modeling we do for children. After all, educators have feelings, too.

Almost every organization, educational and otherwise, harbors a vast emotional undercurrent, a shadowy hidden world of unexpressed feeling. While on the surface we may appear calm and rational, underneath we are churning with emotions: resentment, jealousy, love, fear, guilt, revulsion, caring, pride, frustration, confusion, and joy.

We spend untold time and energy protecting ourselves from people we don't trust, avoiding problems we're afraid to broach, tiptoeing around performance issues, pretending to accept decisions with which we disagree, accepting jobs and assignments we don't want, and withholding our opinions and insights. What a waste. Emotions can help solve problems. Let's use them.

Emotional energy, whether positive or negative, moves us to action. Emotions are the source of passion, motivation, and commitment. When we share our feelings and opinions, work and work relationships are experienced as more vital and meaningful, and movement toward goals accelerates.

We must do everything we can to build schools where feelings are recognized, communication flows freely, and conflicts are handled productively. Where we can air complaints honestly, knowing that they will be viewed as helpful, where diversity is valued and nourished, and inclusion and interdependence are experienced at many levels.

The brightest futures belong to students who develop EQ along with IQ, and to school communities whose citizens have the courage to risk being human in the classroom, lunchroom, office, playground, workroom, and playing field.

When we *model* emotional intelligence, we employ the most potent teaching strategy of all.

EQ Super Strategy: The Sharing Circle

To achieve its goals, *50 Activities for Teaching Emotional Intelligence* incorporates a variety of proven instructional strategies. Activities include simulations, role plays, "experience sheets" for individual students to complete, and a host of small and large group experiments and discussions.

One of the most powerful and versatile of the instructional strategies used in this curriculum is the Sharing Circle. In each unit, two Sharing Circles are fully elaborated. These are followed by a list of additional Sharing Circle topics relevant to the unit topic. At first glance, the Sharing Circle — a small-group discussion process — is likely to appear deceptively simple. It is not. When used correctly, the Sharing Circle is unusually effective as a tool for developing self-awareness, the ability to understand and manage feelings, self-concept, personal responsibility, empathy, communication and group interaction skills.

The Sharing Circle is an ideal way to incorporate emotional learning in the classroom on a regular basis, and helps to form the four building blocks suggested by brain-based education experts Joan Caulfield and Wayne Jennings (see page 14). First, the Sharing Circle provides safety, security, unconditional love and nurturing to each child. Second, Sharing Circle structure and procedures constitute a marked departure from traditional classroom teaching/learning approaches. Topics are stimulating in their ability to provoke self-inquiry. The ambiance is close yet respectful, over time causing intrapersonal defenses and interpersonal barriers to shrink and leading to new levels of group cohesiveness and creativity. Third, circle topics address real-life experiences and issues and the full range of emotions associated with them. And finally, the immediacy of the circle ensures that every child's contributions are heard and accepted on the spot. The attentiveness of other circle members along with their verbal and nonverbal emotional and cognitive reactions constitute a legitimate and powerful form of affirming feedback.

Please take the time to read the following sections before leading your first circle. Once you are familiar with the process, implement Sharing Circles regularly and as frequently as you can.

An Overview of the Sharing Circle

Twenty-seven years of teaching the Sharing Circle process to educators world wide have demonstrated the power of the Sharing Circle in contributing to the development of emotional intelligence. To take full advantage of this process there are some things you need to know.

First, the topic elaboration provided under the heading, "Introduce the Topic," in each Sharing Circle is intended as a guide and does not have to be read verbatim. Once you have used Sharing Circles for a while and are feeling comfortable with the process, you will undoubtedly want to substitute your own words of introduction. We are merely providing you with ideas.

In your elaboration, try to use language and examples that are appropriate to the age, ability, and culture of your students. In our examples, we have attempted to be as general as possible; however, those examples may not be the most appropriate for your students.

Second, we strongly urge you to respect the integrity of the sharing and discussion phases of the circle. These two phases are procedurally and qualitatively different, yet of equal importance in promoting awareness, insight, and higher-level thinking in students. The longer you lead Sharing Circles, the more you will appreciate the instructional advantages of maintaining this unique relationship.

All Sharing Circle topics are intended to develop awareness and insight through voluntary sharing. The discussion questions allow students to understand what has been shared at deeper levels, to evaluate ideas that have been generated by the topic, and to apply specific concepts to other areas of learning.

In order for students to lead fulfilling, productive lives, to interact effectively with others, and to become adept at understanding and responding appropriately to the emotions of others, they first need to become aware of themselves and their own emotions. They need to know who they are, how they feel and function, and how they relate to others.

When used regularly, the *process* of the Sharing Circle coupled with its *content* (specific discussion topics) provides students with frequent opportunities to become more aware of their strengths, abilities, and positive qualities. In the Sharing Circle, students are listened to when they express their feelings and ideas, and they learn to listen to each other. The Sharing Circle format provides a framework in which genuine attention and acceptance can be given and received on a consistent basis.

By sharing their experiences and feelings in a safe environment, students are able to see basic commonalties among human beings — and individual differences, too. This understanding contributes to the development of self-respect. On a foundation of self-respect, students grow to understand and respect others.

As an instructional tool, the purpose of the Sharing Circle is to promote growth and development in students of all ages. Targeted growth areas include communication, self-awareness, personal mastery, and interpersonal skills. As students follow the rules and relate to each other verbally during the Sharing Circle,

they are practicing oral communication and learning to listen. Through insights developed in the course of pondering and discussing the various topics, students are offered the opportunity to grow in awareness and to feel more masterful — more in control of their feelings, thoughts, and behaviors. Through the positive experience of give and take, they learn more about effective modes of social interaction.

The Value of Listening

Many of us do not realize that merely listening to students talk can be immensely facilitating to their personal development. We do not need to diagnose, probe, or problem solve to help students focus attention on their own needs and use the information and insights in their own minds to arrive at their own conclusions. Because being listened to gives students confidence in their ability to positively affect their own lives, listening is certainly the facilitative method with the greatest long-term payoff.

When a student is dealing with a problem, or when her emotional state clearly indicates that something is bothering her, active listening is irreplaceable as a means of helping.

The Sharing Circle provides the opportunity for students to talk while others actively listen. By being given this opportunity, students gain important self-knowledge. Once they see that we do not intend to change them and that they may speak freely without threat of being "wrong," students find it easier to examine themselves and begin to see areas where they can make positive change in their lives. Just through the consistent process of sharing in a safe environment, students develop the ability to clarify their feelings and thoughts. They are encouraged to go deeper, find their own direction, and express and face strong feelings that may at other times be hidden obstacles to their growth. The important point is that students really can solve their own problems, develop self-awareness, and learn skills that will enable them to become responsible members of society if they are listened to effectively.

Awareness

Words are the only tool we have for systematically turning our attention and awareness to the feelings within us, and for describing and reflecting on our thoughts and behaviors. Feelings, after all, lead people to marry, to seek revenge, to launch war, to create great works of art, and to commit their lives to the service of others. They are vital and compelling.

For students to be able to manage their feelings, they must know what those feelings are. To know what they are, they must practice describing them in words. When a particular feeling is grasped in words several times, the mind soon begins to automatically recall ideas and concepts in association with the feeling and can start to provide ways of dealing with the feeling; e.g., "I'm feeling angry and I need to get away from this situation to calm down."

With practice, the mind becomes more and more adept at making these connections. When a recognized feeling comes up, the mind can sort through alternative responses to the feeling. As a student practices this response sequence in reaction to a variety of feelings, he will find words floating into consciousness that accurately identify what is going on emotionally and physically for him. This knowledge in turn develops the capacity to think before and during action. One mark of high emotional intelligence is the ability to recognize one's feelings and to take appropriate, responsible action. The lower a student's EQ, the more often emotional hijackings will determine her behavior. The ability to put words to feelings, to understand those words, to sort through an internal repertoire of responses and to choose appropriate, responsible behavior in reaction to a feeling indicates a high level of self-awareness and emotional intelligence.

By verbally exploring their own experiences in the circle and listening to others do the same, all in an environment of safety, students are gently and gradually prompted to explore deeper

within themselves and to grow and expand in their understanding of others. As this mutual sharing takes place, they learn that feelings, thoughts, and behaviors are real and experienced by everyone. They see others succeeding and failing in the same kinds of ways they succeed and fail. They also begin to see each person as unique and to realize that they are unique, too. Out of this understanding, students experience a growing concern for others. A sense of responsibility develops as the needs, problems, values, and preferences of others penetrate their awareness.

Personal Mastery

Personal mastery can be defined as self-confidence together with responsible competence. Self-confidence is believing in oneself as a capable human being. Responsible competence is the willingness to take responsibility for one's actions coupled with the ability to demonstrate fundamental human relations skills (competencies).

Through participation in Sharing Circles, students are encouraged to explore their successes and hear positive comments about their efforts. Many Sharing Circle topics heighten students' awareness of their own successes and those of others. Failure, or falling short, is a reality that is also examined. The focus, however, is not to remind students that they have failed; instead these topics enable students to see that falling short is common and universal and is experienced by all people when they strive to accomplish things.

Sharing circle topics often address human relations competencies, such as the ability to include others, assume and share responsibility, offer help, behave assertively, solve problems, resolve conflicts, etc. Such topics elevate awareness in the human relations domain and encourage students to more effectively exercise these competencies and skills each day. The first step in a student's developing any competency is knowing that he or she is capable of demonstrating it. The Sharing Circle is particularly adept at helping students to recognize and acknowledge their own capabilities.

A particularly important element of personal mastery is personal responsibility. By focusing on their positive behaviors and accomplishments, the attention of students is directed toward the internal and external rewards that can be gained when they behave responsibly.

The Sharing Circle is a wonderful tool for teaching cooperation. As equitably as possible, the circle structure attempts to meet the needs of all participants. Everyone's feelings are accepted. Comparisons and judgments are not made. The circle is not another competitive arena, but is guided by a spirit of collaboration. When students practice fair, respectful interaction with one another, they benefit from the experience and are likely to employ these responsible behaviors in other life situations.

Interpersonal Skills

Relating effectively to others is a challenge we all face. People who are effective in their social interactions have the ability to understand others. They know how to interact flexibly, skillfully, and responsibly. At the same time, they recognize their own needs and maintain their own integrity. Socially effective people can process the nonverbal as well as verbal messages of others. They possess the very important awareness that all people have the power to affect one another. They are aware of not only how others affect them, but the effects their behaviors have on others.

The Sharing Circle process has been designed so that healthy, responsible behaviors are modeled by the teacher or counselor in his or her role as circle leader. The rules also require that the students relate positively and effectively to one another. The Sharing Circle brings out and affirms the positive qualities inherent in everyone and allows students to practice effective modes of communication. Because Sharing Circles provide a place where participants are listened to and their feelings accepted, students learn how to provide the same conditions to peers and adults outside the circle.

One of the great benefits of the Sharing Circle is that it does not merely teach young people about social interaction, it lets them interact! Every Sharing Circle is a real-life experience of social interaction where the students share, listen, explore, plan, dream, and problem solve together. As they interact, they learn about each other and they realize what it takes to relate effectively to others. Any given Sharing Circle may provide a dozen tiny flashes of positive interpersonal insight for an individual participant. Gradually, the reality of what constitutes effective behavior in relating to others is internalized.

Through this regular sharing of interpersonal experiences, the students learn that behavior can be positive or negative, and sometimes both at the same time. Consequences can be constructive, destructive, or both. Different people respond differently to the same event. They have different feelings and thoughts. The students begin to understand what will cause what to happen; they grasp the concept of cause and effect; they see themselves affecting others and being affected by others.

The ability to make accurate interpretations and responses in social interactions allows students to know where they stand with themselves and with others. They can tell what actions "fit" a situation. Sharing circles are marvelous testing grounds where students can observe themselves and others in action, and can begin to see themselves as contributing to the good and bad feelings of others. With this understanding, students are helped to conclude that being responsible towards others feels good, and is the most valuable and personally rewarding form of interaction.

How to Set Up Sharing Circles

Group Size and Composition

Sharing Circles are a time for focusing on individuals' contributions in an unhurried fashion. For this reason, each circle group needs to be kept relatively small — eight to twelve usually works best. Once they move beyond the primary grades, students are capable of extensive verbalization. You will want to encourage this, and not stifle them because of time constraints.

Each group should be as heterogeneous as possible with respect to sex, ability, and racial/ethnic background. Sometimes there will be a group in which all the students are particularly reticent to speak. At these times, bring in an expressive student or two who will get things going. Sometimes it is necessary for practical reasons to change the membership of a group. Once established, however, it is advisable to keep a group as stable as possible.

Length and Location of Circles

Most circle sessions last approximately 20 to 30 minutes. At first students tend to be reluctant to express themselves fully because they do not yet know that the circle is a safe place. Consequently your first sessions may not last more than 10 to 15 minutes. Generally speaking, students become comfortable and motivated to speak with continued experience.

In middle-school classrooms circle sessions may be conducted at any time during the class period. Starting circle sessions at the beginning of the period allows additional time in case students become deeply involved in the topic. If you start circles late in the period, make sure the students are aware of their responsibility to be concise.

In elementary classes, any time of day is appropriate for Sharing Circles. Some teachers like to set the tone for the day by beginning with circles; others feel it's a perfect way to complete the day and to send the children away with positive feelings.

Circle sessions may be carried out wherever there is room for students to sit in a circle and experience few or no distractions. Most leaders prefer to have students sit in chairs rather than on the floor. Students seem to be less apt to invade one another's space while seated in chairs. Some leaders conduct sessions outdoors, with students seated in a secluded, grassy area.

How to Get Started

Teachers and counselors have used numerous methods to involve students in the circle process. What works well for one leader or class does not always work for another. Here are two basic strategies leaders have successfully used to get groups started. Whichever you use, we recommend that you post a chart listing the circle session rules and procedures to which every participant may refer.

1. Start one group at a time, and cycle through all groups. If possible, provide an opportunity for every student to experience a circle session in a setting where there are no disturbances. This may mean arranging for another staff member or aide to take charge of the students not participating in the circle. Non-participants may work on course work or silent reading, or, if you have a cooperative librarian, they may be sent to the library to work independently or in small groups on a class assignment. Repeat this procedure until all of the students have been involved in at least one circle session.

Next, initiate a class discussion about the circle sessions. Explain that from now on you will be meeting with each circle group in the classroom, with the remainder of the class present. Ask the students to help you plan established procedures for the remainder of the class to follow.

Meet with each circle session group on a different day, systematically cycling through the groups.

2. Combine inner and outer circles. Meet with one circle session group while another group listens and observes as an outer circle. Then have the two groups change places, with the students on the outside becoming the inner circle, and responding verbally to the topic. If you run out of time in middle-school classrooms, use two class periods for this. Later, a third group may be added to this alternating cycle. The end product of this arrangement is two or more groups (comprising everyone in the class) meeting together simultaneously. While one group is involved in discussion, the other groups listen and observe as members of an outer circle. Invite the members of the outer circle to participate in the review and discussion phases of the circle.

Managing the Rest of the Class

A number of arrangements can be made for students who are not participating in circle sessions. Here are some ideas:

- Arrange the room to ensure privacy. This may involve placing a circle of chairs or carpeting in a corner, away from other work areas. You might construct dividers from existing furniture, such as bookshelves or screens, or simply arrange chairs and tables in such a way that the circle area is protected from distractions.

- Involve aides, counselors, parents, or fellow teachers. Have an aide conduct a lesson with the rest of the class while you meet with a circle group. If you do not have an aide assigned to you, use auxiliary staff or parent volunteers.

- Have students work quietly on subject-area assignments in pairs or small, task-oriented groups.

- Utilize student aides or leaders. If the seat-work activity is in a content area, appoint students who show ability in that area as "consultants," and have them assist other students.

- Give the students plenty to do. List academic activities on the board. Make materials for quiet individual activities available so that students cannot run out of things to do and be tempted to consult you or disturb others.

- Make the activity of students outside the circle enjoyable. When you can involve the rest of the class in something meaningful to them, students will probably be less likely to interrupt the circle.

- Have the students work on an ongoing project. When they have a task in progress, students can simply resume where they left off, with little or no introduction from you. In these cases, appointing a "person in charge," "group leader," or "consultant" is wise.

- Allow individual journal-writing. While a circle is in progress, have the other students make entries in a private (or share-with-teacher-only) journal. The topic for journal writing could be the same topic that is being discussed in the Sharing Circle. Do not correct the journals but, if you read them, be sure to respond to the entries with your own written thoughts, where appropriate.

Leading the Sharing Circle

This section is a thorough guide for conducting Sharing Circles. It covers major points to keep in mind and answers questions which will arise as you begin using the program. Please remember that these guidelines are presented to assist you, not to restrict you. Follow them and trust your own leadership style at the same time.

Sharing Circle Procedures for the Leader

1. Setting up the circle (1-2 minutes)

2. Reviewing the ground rules (1-2 minutes) *

3. Introducing the topic (1-2 minutes)

4. Sharing by circle members (12-18 minutes)

5. Reviewing what is shared (3-5 minutes) **

6. Summary discussion (2-8 minutes)

7. Closing the circle (less than 1 minute)

*optional after the first few sessions

**optional

Introducing the topic (1-2 minutes)

State the topic in your own words. Elaborate and provide examples as each activity suggests. Add clarifying statements of your own that will help the students understand the topic. Answer questions about the topic, and emphasize that there are no "right" responses. Finally, restate the topic, opening the session to responses (theirs and yours). Sometimes taking your turn first helps the students understand the aim of the topic. At various points throughout the session, state the topic again.

Just prior to leading a circle session, contemplate the topic and think of at least one possible response that you can make during the sharing phase.

Setting up the circle (1-2 minutes)

As you sit down with the students in the circle, remember that you are not teaching a lesson. You are facilitating a group of people. Establish a positive atmosphere. In a relaxed manner, address each student by name, using eye contact and conveying warmth. An attitude of seriousness blended with enthusiasm will let the students know that the circle session is an important learning experience — an activity that can be interesting and meaningful.

Reviewing the ground rules (1-2 minutes).

At the beginning of the first session, and at appropriate intervals thereafter, go over the rules for the circle session. They are shown at the right.

From this point on, demonstrate to the students that you expect them to remember and abide by the ground rules. Convey that you think well of them and know they are fully capable of responsible behavior. Let them know that by coming to the session they are making a commitment to listen and show acceptance and respect for the other students and you.

Sharing Circle Rules

1. Bring yourself to the circle and nothing else.

2. Everyone gets a turn to share, including the leader.

3. You can skip your turn if you wish.

4. Listen to the person who is sharing.

5. The time is shared equally.

6. Stay in your own space.

7. There are no interruptions, probing, put-downs, or gossip.

Sharing by circle members (12-18 minutes)

The most important point to remember is this: The purpose of the circle session is to give students an opportunity to express themselves and be accepted for the experiences, thoughts, and feelings they share. Avoid taking the action away from the circle members. They are the stars!

Reviewing what is shared (optional 3-5 minutes)

Besides modeling effective listening (the very best way to teach it) and positively reinforcing students for attentive listening, a review can be used to deliberately improve listening skills in circle members.

Reviewing is a time for reflective listening, when circle members feed back what they heard each other say during the sharing phase of the circle. Besides encouraging effective listening, reviewing provides circle members with additional recognition. It validates their experience and conveys the idea, "you are important," a message we can all profit from hearing often.

To review, a circle member simply addresses someone who shared, and briefly paraphrases what the person said ("John, I heard you say....").

The first few times you conduct reviews, stress the importance of checking with the speaker to see if the review accurately summarized the main things that were shared. If the speaker says, "No," allow him or her to make corrections. Stress, too, the importance of speaking directly to the speaker, using the person's name and the pronoun "you," not "he" or "she." If someone says, "She said that...," intervene as promptly and respectfully as possible and say to the reviewer, "Talk to Betty...Say you." This is very important. The person whose turn is being reviewed will have a totally different feeling when talked *to*, instead of *about*.

Note: Remember that the review is optional and is most effective when used occasionally, not as a part of every circle.

Summary discussion (2-8 minutes)

The summary discussion is the cognitive portion of the circle session. During this phase, the leader asks thought-provoking questions to stimulate free discussion and higher-level thinking. Each circle session in this book includes summary questions; however, at times you may want to formulate questions that are more appropriate to the level of understanding in your group—or to what was actually shared in the circle. If you wish to make connections between the circle session topic and your content area, ask questions that will accomplish that objective and allow the summary discussion to extend longer.

It is important that you not confuse the summary with the review. The review is optional; the summary is not. The summary meets the need of people of all ages to find meaning in what they do. Thus, the summary serves as a necessary culmination to each circle session by allowing the students to clarify the key concepts they gained from the session.

Closing the circle (less than 1 minute).

The ideal time to end a circle session is when the summary discussion reaches natural closure. Sincerely thank everyone for being part of the circle. Don't thank specific students for speaking, as doing so might convey the impression that speaking is more appreciated than listening alone. Then close the circle by saying, "The circle session is over," or "OK, that ends our session."

More about Sharing Circle Procedures and Rules

The next few paragraphs offer further clarification concerning circle session leadership.

Why should students bring themselves to the circle and nothing else? Individual teachers differ on this point, but most prefer that students not bring objects (such as pencils, books, etc.) to the circle that may be distracting.

Who gets to talk? Everyone. The importance of acceptance in Sharing Circles cannot be overly stressed. In one way or another practically every ground rule says one thing: accept one another. When you model acceptance of students, they will learn how to be accepting. Each individual in the circle is important and deserves a turn to speak if he or she wishes to take it. Equal opportunity to become involved should be given to everyone in the circle.

Circle members should be reinforced equally for their contributions. There are many reasons why a leader may become more enthused over what one student shares than another. The response may be more on target, reflect more depth, be more entertaining, be philosophically more in keeping with one's own point of view, and so on. However, students need to be given equal recognition for their contributions, even if the contribution is to listen silently throughout the session.

In most of the circle sessions, plan to take a turn and address the topic, too. Students usually appreciate it very much and learn a great deal when their teachers and counselors are willing to tell about their own experiences, thoughts, and feelings. In this way you let your students know that you acknowledge your own humanness.

Does everyone have to take a turn? No. Students may choose to skip their turns. If the circle becomes a pressure situation in which the members are coerced in any way to speak, it will become an unsafe place where participants are not comfortable. Meaningful discussion is unlikely in such an atmosphere. By allowing students to make this choice, you are showing them that you accept their right to remain silent if that is what they choose to do.

As you begin circles, it will be to your advantage if one or more students decline to speak. If you are imperturbable and accepting when this happens, you let them know you are offering them an opportunity to experience something you think is valuable, or at least worth a try, and not attempting to force-feed them. You as a leader should not feel compelled to share a personal experience in every session, either. However, if you decline to speak in most of the sessions, this may have an inhibiting effect on the students' willingness to share.

A word should also be said about how this ground rule has sometimes been carried to extremes. Sometimes leaders have bent over backwards to let students know they don't have to take a turn. This seeming lack of enthusiasm on the part of the leader has caused reticence in the students. In order to avoid this outcome, don't project any personal insecurity as you lead the session. Be confident in your proven ability to work with students. Expect something to happen and it will.

Some circle leaders ask the participants to raise their hands when they wish to speak, while others simply allow free verbal sharing without soliciting the leader's permission first. Choose the procedure that works best for you, but do not call on anyone unless you can see signs of readiness.

Some leaders have reported that their first circles fell flat—that no one, or just one or two students, had anything to say. But they continued to have circles, and at a certain point everything changed. Thereafter, the students had a great deal to say that these leaders considered worth waiting for. It appears that in these cases the leaders' acceptance of the right to skip turns was a key factor. In time most students will contribute verbally when they have something they want to say, and when they are assured there is no pressure to do so.

Sometimes a silence occurs during a circle session. Don't feel you have to jump in every time someone stops talking. During silences students have an opportunity to think about what they would like to share or to contemplate an important idea they've heard. A general rule of thumb is to allow silence to the point that you observe group discomfort. At that point move on. Do not switch to another topic. To do so implies you will not be satisfied until the students speak. If you change to another topic, you are telling them you didn't really mean it when you said they didn't have to take a turn if they didn't want to.

If you are bothered about students who attend a number of circles and still do not share verbally, reevaluate what you consider to be involvement. Participation does not necessarily mean talking. Students who do not speak are listening and learning.

How can I encourage effective listening?

The Sharing Circle is a time (and place) for students and leaders to strengthen the habit of listening by doing it over and over again. No one was born knowing how to listen effectively to others. It is a skill like any other that gets better as it is practiced. In the immediacy of the circle session, the members become keenly aware of the necessity to listen, and most students respond by expecting it of one another.

In the Sharing Circle, listening is defined as the respectful focusing of attention on individual speakers. It includes eye contact with the speaker and open body posture. It eschews interruptions of any kind. When you conduct a circle session, listen and encourage listening in the students by (1) focusing your attention on the person who is speaking, (2) being receptive to what the speaker is saying (not mentally planning your next remark), and (3) recognizing the speaker when she finishes speaking, either verbally ("Thanks, Shirley") or nonverbally (a nod and a smile).

To encourage effective listening in the students, reinforce them by letting them know you have noticed they were listening to each other and you appreciate it. Occasionally conducting a review after the sharing phase also has the effect of sharpening listening skills.

How can I ensure the students get equal time?

When circle members share the time equally, they demonstrate their acceptance of the notion that everyone's contribution is of equal importance. It is not uncommon to have at least one dominator in a group. This person is usually totally unaware that by continuing to talk he or she is taking time from others who are less assertive.

Be very clear with the students about the purpose of this ground rule. Tell them at the outset how much time there is and whether or not you plan to conduct a review. When it is your turn, always limit your own contribution. If someone goes on and on, do intervene (dominators need to know what they are doing), but do so as gently and respectfully as you can.

What are some examples of put-downs?
Put-downs convey the message, "You are not okay as you are." Some put-downs are deliberate, but many are made unknowingly. Both kinds are undesirable in a Sharing Circle because they destroy the atmosphere of acceptance and disrupt the flow of discussion. Typical put-downs include:

- overquestioning.
- statements that have the effect of teaching or preaching
- advice giving
- one-upsmanship
- criticism, disapproval, or objections
- sarcasm
- statements or questions of disbelief

How can I deal with put-downs? There are two major ways for dealing with put-downs in circle sessions: preventing them from occurring and intervening when they do.

Going over the ground rules with the students at the beginning of each session, particularly in the earliest sessions, is a helpful preventive technique. Another is to reinforce the students when they adhere to the rule. Be sure to use nonpatronizing, nonevaluative language.

Unacceptable behavior should be stopped the moment it is recognized by the leader. When you become aware that a put-down is occurring, do whatever you ordinarily do to stop destructive behavior in the classroom. If one student gives another an unasked-for bit of advice, say for example, "Jane, please give Alicia a chance to tell her story." To a student who interrupts say, "Ed, it's Sally's turn." In most cases the fewer words, the better — students automatically tune out messages delivered as lectures.

Sometimes students disrupt the group by starting a private conversation with the person next to them. Touch the offender on the arm or shoulder while continuing to give eye contact to the student who is speaking. If you can't reach the offender, simply remind him or her of the rule about listening. If students persist in putting others down during circle sessions, ask to see them at another time and hold a brief one-to-one conference, urging them to follow the rules. Suggest that they reconsider their membership in the circle. Make it clear that if they don't intend to honor the ground rules, they are not to come to the circle.

How can I keep students from gossiping?
Periodically remind students that using names and sharing embarrassing information is not acceptable. Urge the students to relate personally to one another, but not to tell intimate details of their lives.

What should the leader do during the summary discussion? Conduct the summary as an open forum, giving students the opportunity to discuss a variety of ideas and accept those that make sense to them. Don't impose your opinions on the students, or allow the students to impose theirs on one another. Ask open-ended questions, encourage higher-level thinking, contribute your own ideas when appropriate, and act as a facilitator.

Bibliography and Resources

Armstrong, Thomas, *In Their Own Way: Discovering and Encouraging Your Child's Personal Learning Style*, Los Angeles: Jeremy P. Tarcher, Inc., 1987.

Arnold, William, W. and Plas, Jeanne M., *The Human Touch: Today's Most Unusual Program for Productivity and Profit*, New York: Wiley, 1993.

Berry, Diane. S. and Pennebaker, James W., "Nonverbal and Verbal Emotional Expression and Health," *Psychotherapy and Psychosomatics*, Vol 59, 1993.

Brody, Leslie R. and Hall, Judith A., "Gender and Emotion," *Handbook of Emotions*, New York: Guilford Press, 1993.

Caulfield, Joan and Jennings, Wayne, "Emotional Aspect of Brain Recognized," *Networker*, Winter 1996.

Cowan, David, *Taking Charge of Organizational Conflict*, Spring Valley, California: Innerchoice Publishing, 1995.

Davidson, Richard, *The Nature of Emotion: Fundamental Questions*, New York and Oxford: Oxford University Press, 1995.

Dreikers, Rudolf, *Psychodynamics and Counseling*, Chicago: Adler School of Professional Psychology, 1967.

Evans, Phil, *Motivation and Emotion*, London: Routledge, 1989.

Francis, Martha E. and Pennebaker, James W., "Talking and Writing as Illness Prevention." *Medicine, Exercise, Nutrition and Health*, American Journal of Health Promotion, Vol. 6, Issue 4, 1992.

Gardner, Howard, *Frames of Mind: The Theory of Multiple Intelligences*, New York: Basic Books, 1983.

Goleman, Daniel, *Emotional Literacy: A Field Report*, Fetzer Institute of Dalamazoo, Michigan, 1996.

Goleman, Daniel, "Emotional Intelligence: Why It Can Matter More Than IQ," *Learning*, May/June, 1996.

Goleman, Daniel, *Emotional Literacy: Why It Can Matter More Than IQ*, New York: Bantam, 1995.

Humphry, Nicholas, *A History of the Mind: Evolution and the Birth of Consciousness*, New York: Simon and Schuster, 1992.

Lazarus, Richard S., *Passion and Reason: Making Sense of Our Emotions*, New York and Oxford: Oxford Universaity Press, 1994.

Levenson, Robert W, "Human Emotion: A Functional View," *The Nature of Emotion: Fundamental Questions*, Oxford University Press, 1995.

Ralston, Faith, *Hidden Dynamics: How Emotions Affect Business Performance*, New York: American Management Association, 1995.

Richards, Dick, *Artful Work: Awakening Joy, Meaning, and Commitment in the Workplace*, San Francisco: Berrett-Koehler Publishers, 1995.

Saarni, Carolyn, "Emotional Competence: How Emotions and Relationships Become Integrated," in Thompson, R.A., *Socioemtional Development*, Lincoln and London: University of Nebraska Press, 1990.

Salovey, Peter, and Mayer, John D., "Emotional Intelligence," *Imagination, Cognition, and Personality 9*, 1990.

Solomon, Robert C., *The Passions: Emotions and the Meaning of Life*, Indianapolis and Cambridge: Hacket Publishing Company, 1993.

Vail, Priscilla, "The On Off Switch for Learning," *Connections: The Newletter of Social and Emotional Learning*, Collaborative for the Advancement of Social and Emotional Learning, Yale University, 1994.

Self-awareness

Activities in this unit teach students to:

- recognize their individual interests, abilities, strengths, and weaknesses.

- examine the values and individual differences that help determine their favorite activities.

- acknowledge the personal values, treasured experiences, and important relationships that give significance to symbolic objects.

Sharing Circles in this unit allow students to:

- describe a favorite possession and discuss what gives material items emotional as well as monetary value.

- describe activities they particularly enjoy and the feelings generated by participation in those activities.

This Is Me!
Experience Sheet and Discussion

Objectives:

The students will:

—identify individual interests, abilities, strengths, and weaknesses.

—define individual differences as contributing to personal uniqueness.

Materials:

one copy of the experience sheet, "This is Me!," for each student

Procedure:

Show the students the experience sheet. Read the directions to them. Explain that they will have about 10 minutes to complete the experience sheet, and will then be asked to join you for a discussion. Tell the students that it will be interesting to find out what they think about themselves. Distribute the copies of the experience sheet and, if possible, circulate as the students complete them. Offer assistance as needed. Lead a follow-up discussion.

Discussion Questions

1. Which words did you choose to describe yourself?
2. What are some of the things that you enjoy doing?
3. What are some of the things that you do well?
4. Do our experience sheets look different from one another? Why is that?
5. Why is it important to get to know ourselves and each other in ways like this?

This Is Me!
Experience Sheet

1. Draw a red circle around words that describe you.
2. Draw a blue circle around words that name things you enjoy doing.
3. Draw a green circle around words that name things you do well.
   It's okay to draw more than one circle around the same word.

drawing	girl	having a pet
running	helping at home	gardening
using a computer	short	cooking
brown hair	reading	collecting things
chocolate milk	blonde bair	carrots
dancing	acting	tall
doing puzzles	listening to music	flowers
talking with friends	brown skin	pony tail
green eyes	wear glasses	tennis shoes
friendly	writing	yogurt
boy	freckles	kittens
arithmetic	hula hoops	going barefoot
ice cream	computer games	curly hair
science	painting	_____
swimming	helping at school	_____
playing a musical instrument	red hair	_____
		_____

Find the Secret Message!
Self-Discovery Through Puzzles

Objectives:

The students will:

—graphically convey information about themselves.

—identify a present or future activity that is important to them.

—describe emotions that move them to perform valued activities.

Materials:

For each puzzle: one sheet of tag or poster board, crayons or colored markers, scissors, pencil, and a flat box approximately 9 inches by 12 inches

Procedure:

Give each student a piece of tag or poster board and crayons or markers.

Ask the students to take a few moments to think of an activity that is important to them. The activity can be something they do presently or something they plan to do (or dream about doing) in the future. Then have the students draw and color that image on the tag board, filling the sheet from edge to edge.

Next, tell the students to turn the picture over and write a secret message on the other side. The message can explain the importance of the activity they illustrated, or it can describe a personal trait, interest, hobby, or goal. Tell the students to be sure to include their name in the message.

Distribute scissors and have the students cut their picture into large puzzle pieces. Demonstrate this process for older students. For younger students, either provide assistance or collect the pictures and make the puzzles yourself, later. When the students have completed their puzzles, lead a follow-up discussion.

Store each puzzle in a flat box at a learning center or special interest area. To find the secret message, a student fits the puzzle together in the box, puts the lid on the box, turns the box over and lifts the bottom away from the lid. If the puzzle is assembled correctly, the message will be visible.

Discussion Questions:

1. How difficult was it to choose an activity to illustrate?
2. How do you know that something is important to you?
3. What feelings do you have inside when you think about doing something you enjoy or consider important?
4. Without revealing your secret message, what did you learn about yourself from doing this activity?

It's In the Bag
Speaking/Collecting Activity

Objectives:

The students will:

—select and share items that have special meaning to them.

—identify and describe aspects of themselves and their lives.

Materials:

'Me' bags (one per child) containing things that represent the children's interests.

Procedure:

One class session before this activity, ask the students to gather pictures, treasures, and memorabilia, place them in a brown paper bag, and bring the bag to the next class. Show them an example, by displaying a bag of your own memorabilia.

Have the students form a circle with their bags in front of them. Ask for volunteers, or draw names, to determine the order of sharing.

In your own words, explain the activity: *Pick items from your bag, show them, and tell the group what each is and why it is important to you. Tell us if the item is something you like or dislike, and how you came to have this thing. For example, you might explain that you brought ticket stubs from a special movie or concert you attended. Or you might show a picture of a ballerina because you want to take dance lessons and would like to be a performer someday.*

Some of the students may need a little prompting from you during the sharing process. When a student is shy or reluctant, ask questions like, "Was that a gift?" or "Would you like to tell us why that is important to you?"

After the sharing, have the students return to their regular seating. Lead a brief follow-up discussion.

Discussion Questions:

1. How did you feel when you were sharing your treasures and memorabilia?
2. Did anyone include items that represent things they do *not* enjoy or that give them *bad* feelings? Why?
3. What do you think your bag of treasures says about you? What message does it convey?

One of My Favorite Possessions
A Sharing Circle

Objectives:
The students will:
—identify and describe a valued possession.
—explain the nature and source of their feelings about the item.

Introduce the Topic:
All of us have possessions that we prize and value highly. We enjoy using them or perhaps we get pleasure from just looking at them. Today, we'll each have an opportunity to talk about something that is very special to us. Our topic is, "One of My Favorite Possessions."

You probably own several things that are special to you. You may have had some of these possessions since you were very young, and you have probably acquired others more recently. Tell us about one special thing you own, and describe what makes that item important to you. Someone you care for very much may have given it to you, or you may have done extra chores to earn enough money to buy it. The item could be something that's fun to wear, or play with, or work with. Or it might be an item that simply looks nice in your room. Think about it for a moment. The topic is, "One of My Favorite Possessions."

Discussion Questions:
1. What is it that makes certain things special to us?
2. Do you think it's important for people to have favorite possessions? Why or Why not?
3. What did you learn about yourself or another person during this circle?

Something I Really Like To Do
A Sharing Circle

Objectives:

The students will:

—describe a preferred activity.

—explain the feelings associated from a preferred activity.

—trace some of the sources of their likes, dislikes, and personal preferences.

State the topic:

Our topic for today is "Something I Really Like To Do." There are probably many things that you like to do. However, today I'd like you to pick just one activity that you truly enjoy and tell us about it. Perhaps drawing pictures is a favorite activity of yours, or writing stories, or playing computer games. Maybe you enjoy swimming, dancing, or building models. Take a moment to think about it. When you're ready to share, raise your hand and tell us about "Something I Really Like To Do."

Discussion Questions

1. What were the different activities mentioned in the circle?
2. What determines whether you enjoy an activity or not?
3. Why do people like to do different things?
4. Where or how do we acquire our likes and dislikes?

Additional Sharing Circle Topics

A Person I Admire

A Secret Wish I Have

Something I Like to Do Alone

The Craziest Dream I Ever Had

One Way I Wish I Could Be Different

An Important Event in My Life

Something I Want to Keep

Something I Like to Do with Others

When I Felt Comfortable Just Being Me

Something I Need Help With

My Favorite Place

My Idea of a Perfect Saturday Afternoon

Something About My Culture That I Appreciate

The Funniest Thing That Ever Happened to Me

My Favorite Vacation

Something I Like to Do With My Family

My Favorite Daydream

One of the Best Things That Ever Happened to Me

Something About Me That You Wouldn't Know Unless I Told You

A Friend of Mine Who Is Different From Me

Something I Really Like to Do at School

If I Had One Wish It Would Be

One Way I Wish I Could Be Different

One Thing I Am Sure I Can Do Well

Something I Want

A Special Occasion or Holiday Related to My Culture

A Person I'd Like to Be Like

Managing Feelings

Activities in this unit teach students to:

- develop and practice a vocabulary for feelings.

- identify facial expressions and other nonverbal behaviors associated with specific feelings.

- identify situations and people that make them angry, and develop constructive ways of dealing with anger.

Sharing Circles in this unit allow students to:

- describe incidents that caused them to feel happiness and discuss the effects happy feelings have on work and play.

- describe sad experiences, recognize that sadness is normal, and discuss ways of lifting their spirits when they are down.

The Write Stuff
A Vocabulary for Feelings

Objectives:
The students will:
—acquaint themselves with a variety of feelings words and their meanings.
—demonstrate an understanding of new feeling words.

Materials:
one copy of the experience sheet, "So Many Ways to Feel" for each student; writing paper and pencils

Procedure:
Begin by asking the students to help you brainstorm words that describe feelings. Cover the board with these words.

Ask volunteers to choose a word from the list and describe a real or hypothetical situation that causes them to feel this way. For example, a student who chooses the word "exasperated," might explain that having to pick up a younger sister's dirty clothes makes her feel exasperated.

After many students have shared their situations using the words on the board, distribute the experience sheets. Give the students several minutes to look over the words, and then ask volunteers to name those that are unfamiliar. Discuss the meaning of the words with the entire group.

Explain to the students that they are going to have an opportunity to practice using words from the list that they have not previously used. Ask the students to choose 5 words from the list, and to use these words in five sentences — one sentence demonstrating a correct meaning and context for each word. Tell the students that they may use any of the following suggestions in creating their sentences:

1. Use a sentence pattern: "I feel/felt (new feeling word) when (something happens/happened)."

2. If possible, change a word to an adverb by adding *ly* and use it to describe an action: "I jealously watched as my opponent received the gold medal in the 100 yard dash."

3. Use the word in a sentence that tells why someone feels/felt that way: "The miserable woman trudged another five miles through the snow looking for a service station where she could buy gas for her stalled car."

When the students have completed their sentences, ask them to form dyads and to read their sentences to their partner. Invite the partners to give each other feedback — for example, which sentence they liked best and why. Then gather the group together and invite volunteers to share a sentence. Finish with a general discussion.

Discussion Questions:
1. Why is it beneficial to know lots of feeling words?
2. What good does it do to have so many words to describe similar feelings?
3. Which words on the list have you felt before, without knowing their names? Which words have you known before, without ever experiencing the feeling?

So Many Ways to Feel
Experience Sheet

abandoned	depressed	grateful	judgmental	repulsive
accepted	deprived	gratified	jumpy	restless
adamant	desperate	greedy		restrained
adequate	destructive	grieving	lazy	
affectionate	determined	groovy	left out	sad
afraid	different	guilty	lonely	satisfied
agonized	diffident	gullible	loser, like a	scared
alarmed	diminished	gutles	lovable	screwed up
alienated	disappointed		loving	settled
ambivalent	discontented	happy	low	shallow
annoyed	distracted	hateful	loyal	shocked
anxious	distraught	helpful		shy
apathetic	disturbed	helpless	manipulated	silly
appreciated	divided	high	miserable	sluggish
astounded	dominated	homesick	misunderstood	sorry
attractive	dubious	honored		spiritual
awed		hopeful	needy	strained
awkward	eager	hopeless	nervous	stunned
	ecstatic	horrible	nice	stupid
bad	elated	hostile		sure
beaten	electrified	hurt	odd	
beautiful	embarrassed	hysterical	opposed	tempted
betrayed	empty		optimistic	tense
bewildered	enchanted	ignored	outraged	threatened
bitter	energetic	immobilized	overlooked	thwarted
blissful	envious	impatient	overwhelmed	tired
bold	evasive	imposed upon		torn
bored	exasperated	impressed	panicked	touched
brave	excited	inadequate	paranoid	touchy
burdened	exhausted	incompetent	peaceful	trapped
	exhilarated	in control	persecuted	troubled
comfortable		indecisive	petrified	
concerned	fawning	independent	pleasant	unappreciated
confident	fearful	infatuated	pleased	uncertain
connected	flustered	inferior	possessive	uneasy
cop-out, like a	foolish	infuriated	preoccupied	unsettled
cowardly	frantic	inhibited	pressured	uptight
creative	free	insecure		used
curious	friendless	insincere	quarrelsome	
cut off from others	friendly	inspired	quiet	violent
	frightened	intimidated		vivacious
deceitful	frustrated	involved	refreshed	vulnerable
defeated	full	isolated	rejected	
dejected			relaxed	wishy-washy
delighted	glad	jealous	relieved	wonderful
dependent	good	joyous	remorseful	worried

Feeling Faces
Expressing Feelings with Masks

Objectives:

The students will:
—identify a variety of feelings and associate them with feeling words
—recall and share incidents in which they experienced various feelings.

Materials:

Paper plates, flat wooden sticks (such as tongue depressors or popsicle sticks), scissors, colored markers and/or crayons, and glue

Procedure:

Get the attention of the students and tell them to listen carefully while you read them the poem below. Ask the students to listen for feelings and to remember as many as they can.

Angry at Marty
Loving t'ward Lou
I'm full of feelings
What shall I do?

Proud of my drawing
Jealous of your bike
I show my feelings
And hide them, too

Happy after winning
Sad when I lose
I change my feelings
Like I change my shoes.

Tired in the morning
Hungry at noon
Do you have feelings
That bother you, too?

Depressed by grades
Scared of the dark
Why all these feelings...
What good do they do?

Surprised by mysteries
Amused by cartoons
If you lack feelings
I'll give some to you.

Excited by birthdays
Bored when they're through
I'll understand feelings
In a year or two.

After you have read the poem, ask the students to call out the feeling words that they identified. Point out that it is perfectly normal to experience all of the feelings mentioned and that, while everyone experiences them, each person feels and expresses them a little differently. Jot each word on the board and add others until you have a list that includes:

happy	sad	scared
angry	proud	excited
confused	tired	surprised
bored	amused	jealous
loving	hungry	depressed

Have the students pair up. Distribute the mask-making materials and, in your own words, explain:

You are going to work together to create a mask that shows one of the feelings listed on the board. First, agree on the feeling you want illustrate and then, using colored markers, make a face on the paper plate that depicts that feeling. Exaggerate the features to make the feeling come across as forcefully as possible.

Demonstrate the process, or show the students a mask that you have made in advance. Circulate and help the students cut eye holes in their masks and glue their sticks in place to create handles.

When the masks are finished, have each pair join three other pairs to form circles of eight. Direct the students to take turns holding their mask in front of their face, relating a time when they experienced the feeling shown, and acting out some of the things they did and said to express that feeling. Circulate and coach the students, as necessary, reminding them to pass their mask to their partner after they have had a turn.

Suggest that the masks be displayed around the room and that the students continue to use them throughout the year to aid them in expressing feelings. Conclude the activity with a total group discussion.

Discussion Questions:

1. Which feelings were easiest to express and recognize? Which were hardest? Why do you think that is?
2. How did you feel when you were acting out your situation?
3. Did the mask make it easier to act out your feelings? Why or why not?
4. Why is it important to be aware of and express our feelings?
5. Who decided how you would express your feeling? In real life, who always decides?
5. When you have feelings that make it hard for you to work in school, what can you do to feel better? Whom can you talk to?

Variations:

- Make paper-bag masks, which require large eye holes but no gluing.
- If the group is relatively small, lead the sharing, dramatizations, and discussion in one large circle.
- If time is short, spread the activity over two sessions. Make the masks during the first session; lead the sharing, dramatizations, and discussion during the second.

Things I Get Angry About
Experience Sheet and Discussion

Objectives:
The students will:
—examine people, conditions, and situations that generate anger in them.
—describe appropriate ways to handle or express anger.

Materials:
one copy of the experience sheet, "Things I Get Angry About," for each student; chalkboard and chalk

Procedure:
Begin by involving the students in a brief dialogue on the subject of anger. For example, you might write the word *anger* on the board and ask, "Has anyone felt this emotion today?" allowing two or three volunteers to briefly describe what happened to make them angry. Or you might ask the students to think of other words that describe different levels of anger (irritated, annoyed, furious, etc.), list them, and then talk about how anger builds.

Next, distribute the experience sheets. Ask the students to think about and write down various conditions, situations, and people that cause them anger. Instruct the students to list one or two appropriate ways of handling the anger in each situation.

In a follow-up discussion, invite several volunteers to share one item from their list. Invite the other students to suggest additional ways to handle anger in each of those situations. In the process, make the following points about anger:

• Anger is a basic human emotion and is neither bad nor good.
• Sometimes anger serves a protective function.
• There are healthy and appropriate ways to deal with the anger we feel.
• Each of us is responsible for our own feelings and behavior.
• It is how we react to a situation, not the situation itself, that causes our anger and upset.

Discussion Questions:
1. How does your body feel when you are angry?
2. How can you tell when someone else is angry?
3. Why is it a good idea to find positive ways of dealing with anger?
4. What have you learned about handling anger from this activity?

Things I Get Angry About
Experience Sheet

Many people react angrily to the same things—and the same people—over and over again. What about you? Are there certain things (such as not getting your way or not being listened to) that almost always upset you? List several people and situations that usually make you angry. Then list several things you can do to deal with your feelings of anger.

Situations and People	What I Can Do About My Anger

Something That Makes Me Especially Happy
A Sharing Circle

Objectives:

The students will:

—describe situations or events that inspire feelings of happiness.

—discuss how happy moments affect their functioning and ability to learn.

Introduce the Topic:

Our topic for this session is, "Something That Makes Me Especially Happy." Think about the things you particularly like and tell us about one that almost always makes you happy. It could be something you enjoy doing, eating, or seeing, and it could involve another person — a friend, perhaps. It doesn't have to be anything colossal, just something that causes you to feel happy — even if other people don't feel the same way. Let's take a few moments to think about it quietly. The topic is, "Something That Makes Me Especially Happy."

Discussion Questions:

1. How can you tell when a person is happy?
2. How does your body feel when you are happy?
3. Who decides whether or not something makes you happy? Why do you think that is?
4. How do happy feelings affect your ability to work and play?
5. Is your schoolwork better when you are feeling happy, or when you are feeling unhappy? Why do you think that is?

A Feeling of Sadness I Remember
A Sharing Circle

Objectives:
The students will:
—recall and describe sad experiences.
—discuss causes of and cures for sad feelings.

Introduce the Topic:
Our topic for this session is, "A Feeling of Sadness I Remember." We all feel sad at times. Life regularly presents us with its negative as well as its positive sides.

Can you remember a time when you felt sadness or grief about something? Maybe you lost a relative, a friend, or a pet. Perhaps you saw a homeless person and were struck by the sadness of his or her plight. Or maybe you were moved to sadness by the impact of a movie, a play, or a piece of music. Let's observe a minute of silence and think of times we've experienced sadness. If you decide to share, the topic is, "A Feeling of Sadness I Remember."

Discussion Questions:
1. What lessons, if any, do sad experiences offer us?
2. Is it wise to try to avoid all sad experiences? Why or why not?
3. What is the relationship between sadness and love?
4. What are some things you can do to lift up your feelings when you are sad?

Additional Sharing Circle Topics

A Time I Felt Happy
A Time I Felt Scared
A Time I Felt Unhappy
How I React When I'm Angry
A Time I Couldn't Control My Curiosity
A Time I Got My Feelings Hurt
A Favorite Feeling
Someone Who Respects My Feelings
A Time I Felt Excited
I Felt Good and Bad About the Same Thing
A Time I Handled My Feelings Well
A Secret Fear I Have
Something I Hate to Do
How Somebody Hurt My Feelings
How I Feel When People Tell Me They Like Me
Something in My Life That I'm Happy About
I Could Have Hurt Someone's Feelings, But Didn't
A Feeling I Had a Hard Time Accepting
A Time I Was Alone But Not Lonely
A Thought I Have That Makes Me Feel Happy
A Time When It Was Okay to Express My Feelings
I Told Someone How I Was Feeling
I Did Something Impulsive and Regretted It Later
A Time I Really Controlled My Feelings
A Time I Was Afraid to Do Something But Did It Anyway
A Time I Helped Someone Who Was Afraid
A Time I Was Scared and It Was Fun
A Way I Get Over Being Afraid

Decision Making

Activities in this unit teach students to:

- view decision making as a creative process involving systematic investigation, problem solving, and choosing among alternatives based on established criteria.

- examine their own decision making process by analyzing a variety of recent decisions.

- practice a basic four-step decision-making process.

Sharing Circles in this unit allow students to:

- explore the benefits of participating in decisions that affect them.

- describe situations in which they had to make a choice from two or more undesirable alternatives, and discuss their emotions and behaviors in these situations.

Finding a New Nest
Science Lesson and Role Play

Objectives:

The students will:

—identify simple strategies used in solving problems.

—identify alternatives in decision-making situations.

Materials:

a copy of *The Evolution Book* by Sara Stein, Workman Publishing Company, New York, 1986 (optional); props and costume materials for the role play (optional)

Procedure:

If you can obtain a copy of Sara Stein's *The Evolution Book*, read "Househunting Honeybees" on pages 218-219. This very short, but fascinating article describes the process by which a swarm of honeybees sets out to find a new home — usually in the cavity of a decaying tree. If you do not have the book, don't worry. Here is a summary of the story:

Every honeybee carries in its brain a "plan" for an ideal hive. A few hundred workers, each working individually, scout the countryside for likely sites. They poke into knotholes and among tree roots. When a bee finds a possible site, she checks the dimensions by pacing out the measurements from one end to the other, around the circumference, and to various points from the entrance. She returns to check the same site several times under different weather conditions and at different times of the day. Scouts come together to report their findings in the form of dances. The degree to which a site matches the "ideal" hive is reflected in the enthusiasm of the dance that is used to "sell" it to the other bees. Scouts who have less good news to report dance less vigorously, and may soon join the dance of one of the more enthusiastic bees. In so doing, they learn the location of her site, and fly off to investigate it themselves. If they like it, they return to convert still more scouts and, after several days, a decision is made.

Tell the story to the students in your own words. Simplify the language and dramatize the wonderful ability of the worker bees to achieve their goal through systematic investigation, problem-solving, and decision-making. Demonstrate to the students the size and height of the "ideal" nest. For example, mark the minimum height of a nest (6 1/2 feet from the ground) on a wall or bulletin board, and simulate the capacity of a nest (47 quarts) by showing the students two 5-gallon bottles or some other container or space of about the right size. Involve the students in the story by asking them questions, such as:

—*How would you feel if you were faced with building a new home?*

—*How would you feel if you were expected to go exploring every day?*

—*How would you feel if you had to work alone on such an important assignment?*

Younger students will probably enjoy dramatizing the househunting process. Choose several children to play the part of worker bees hunting for a place to build a new nest. If you have costume materials (antennae, wings, yellow and black striped shirts, etc.) let the children wear them. While you narrate, have the scouts "fly" off in search of possible sites. If you can, have different spaces around the room available and marked for investigation. Direct each scout to measure his space by pacing it off, flying around it, etc. Have the scouts come back together and report their findings in the form of creative dances, with the most enthusiastic dances gradually gaining converts until a decision is made.

Conclude the activity. Point out to the children that the bees made their decision by 1) finding many possible sites (identifying alternatives), 2) comparing the sites to the "ideal" hive (evaluating alternatives), and 3) choosing the best site (selecting an alternative). Lead a culminating discussion.

Discussion Questions:

1. How do bees choose the best place to live?
2. Do you think they make good decisions that way?
3. Why is it important to look at different choices before deciding on one?
4. How do the "feelings" of bees contribute to decision making.
5. How do feelings affect the decisions you make?

Thinking About Decisions
Experience Sheet and Discussion

Objectives:

The students will:

—clarify personal beliefs and attitudes and how these affect decision-making.

—describe how decisions affect self and others.

Materials:

a pencil and one copy of the experience sheet, "Thinking About Decisions," for each student

Procedure:

Distribute the experience sheets. Read the directions to the children while they read along silently. Talk about the different types of decisions and give an example of each.

Have the students complete the experience sheets.

Lead a discussion. Go over the list of decisions on the experience sheet. Ask for a show of hands indicating which of the five categories the students chose for each decision. Discuss the reasons for their choices. Then ask volunteers to tell the group about some of their own decisions described at the bottom of the experience sheet. Facilitate discussion.

Discussion Questions:

1. Were most of your decisions automatic?
2. Were many decisions out of your control?
3. What kinds of decisions do you give a lot of thought?
4. Which decisions were affected by your personal beliefs? Your attitudes?
5. Which decisions were affected by your friends?
6. Which decision were affected by your parents?
7. Which decisions were affected by your interests?
8. What have you learned about decision making from this activity? What have you learned about yourself?

Thinking About Decisions
Experience Sheet

Everyone makes decisions daily. Some of the decisions are more important than others. Some are so important that they require lots of thought and study before a decision is made. Others are automatic. Here are five categories for showing how decisions are made:

0 = Not under my control
1 = Automatic
2 = Sometimes think about it

3 = Think about it, but don't study it
4 = Study it a little bit
5 = Study it a lot

Below is a list of decisions. In front of each, put the number that stands for how you would make the decision:

___ To get up in the morning
___ To tell the truth
___ What books to read
___ To say please and thank you
___ To stop at STOP signs
___ To ride a bicycle
___ Where to throw trash

___ To criticize a friend behind his/her back
___ What to eat and when
___ To study for a test
___ To use drugs
___ What to do when you grow up
___ To go to school
___ What movie to see

Think back over the past week. On the lines below, describe some decisions you have made. Try to include one decision in each of these areas:

• decisions about what to do _____

_____

• decisions about school _____

_____

• common, everyday decisions _____

_____

• health and safety decisions_____

_____

• decisions about what is right and wrong_____

_____

Decisions, Decisions, Decisions!
Teacher Presentation and Discussion

Objectives:

The students will:

—identify alternatives in decision-making situations.

—clarify personal beliefs and attitudes and state how these affect decision-making.

Materials:

chart paper and magic marker or chalkboard and chalk

Procedure:

Introduce the activity. Say to the students: *We all make many decisions every day. Sometimes decisions are easy to make and sometimes they are hard. When they are hard, it helps to know some steps to take in making them. I'm going to read you a story about a girl who has a tough decision to make. Afterwards, let's see if we can figure out what she ought to do.*

Karen and Susan are friends. They sit next to each other at school. Karen is good at math. Susan doesn't like math, and has trouble with it. Tomorrow, their teacher is going to give the class a big math test. Susan comes up to Karen after school. She looks worried. She asks Karen if she can copy her answers on the test tomorrow. Karen doesn't say anything. But at home that night, she worries. She has to decide what to do.

Give the students a few moments to think about the situation. Then ask them:

—*Why is Karen worried?*

—*What decision does Karen have to make?*

—*If Karen lets Susan copy her answers, what could happen?*

—*If Karen says no, what could happen?*

—*If Karen does nothing at all, what could happen?*

—*If you were Karen, would you talk to someone before deciding? Who?*

—*What decision do you think Karen should make?*

During the discussion, you and the children will no doubt name most of the steps in the decision-making process. As they are mentioned, write them on the chart paper.

1. What is the decision about? (definition)
2. What are my choices? (alternatives)
3. What could happen if I make each choice? (consequences)
4. What is the best decision?

Read through the steps with the students and discuss them. Then present additional decision-making situations. Ask the students to pretend that they are the person making the decision. Go through all of the steps together and then ask the students what decision they would make and why. Facilitate discussion throughout and at the conclusion of the activity.

Sample Decision-Making Situations

Rick's uncle is visiting for the weekend. He wants to take Rick out exploring on a big boat. They will be gone all weekend. Rick would have to miss Little League practice. His team is getting ready for the play-offs. He has to make a decision.

Leah likes Carol better than any baby-sitter she's ever had. Carol plays games with Leah and her little brother. She reads to them and is always nice. But last night, when Leah got up to go to the bathroom, she saw Carol pouring herself a glass of wine from the refrigerator. When Carol saw Leah watching, she seemed upset. She said, "Don't tell anyone, okay?"

Greg and Paul ask Ruben to ride his bike to the shopping mall with them. They offer to take him to a movie. Ruben really wants to go, but the brakes on his bike aren't working very well. He could probably make it, but he'd have to ride through heavy traffic. He has to decide what to do.

Discussion Questions:

1. Why is Rick's decision difficult? (He has to decide between two desirable and important activities.)
2. Why is Carol's decision difficult? (She faces a moral dilemma — informing her parents vs. protecting her baby-sitter.)
3. Why is Ruben's decision difficult? (He has to decide whether to risk his own safety for a little fun.)
4. What feelings would you have in Rick's situation? ...in Carol's? ...in Ruben's?
5. Should you trust your feelings when you have a tough decision to make? Why or why not?

When I Got to Share in Making a Decision
A Sharing Circle

Objectives:

The students will:

—describe decision-making processes in which they have participated.

—explain how participating in the process affects their commitment to a decision.

Introduce the Topic:

Today's topic is, "When I Got to Share in Making a Decision." We all like to be part of the decision-making process. We want to help our families plan vacations and decide what movies to see. We want to be involved when our friends decide how to spend Saturday afternoon. When a decision involves us, we want to express our ideas and give our input.

Tell us about a time when you helped make a group decision. You may have helped your parents decide whether or not to sign you up for dance or music lessons. Perhaps you helped make all the decisions required for a Christmas or birthday surprise. Right now, you and your parents may be deciding which sports programs are best for you, or what color to paint the house. It doesn't matter if the decision was big or small; we want to know how you felt and what you learned from the experience. The topic is, "When I Got to Share in Making a Decision."

Discussion Questions:

1. What are the advantages of helping to make decisions that affect you?
2. What do you usually contribute to the decision-making process?
3. How do you feel when you are a part of the decision making process?

A Time I Had to Choose the Best of Two Bad Things
A Sharing Circle

Objectives:

The students will:

—weigh the relative consequences of difficult choices.

—apply universal moral values, such as honesty, respect and responsibility, as standards in decision making.

Introduce the Topic:

Have you ever been in a situation where you had to make a choice and it seemed like someone would get hurt no matter what you chose to do? Decisions like that are very difficult, but we all have to make them occasionally.

Maybe you had to choose between telling the truth and protecting a friend. If you told the truth, it would get your friend in trouble, but to protect your friend, you had to lie. Or maybe your mom asked if you liked the new clothes she bought for you. You didn't really like them or want to wear them, but you hated to hurt her feelings. Perhaps your family had to decide whether to allow a sick or injured pet to continue living — and suffering — or have it put to sleep. Have you ever done something you didn't really want to do rather than hurt a friend's feelings or risk losing a friendship? When both choices look bad, choosing seems like losing. And sometimes being honest is very tough. Think this over for a few moments. The topic is, "A Time I Had to Choose the Best of Two Bad Things."

Discussion Questions:

1. How do you feel when you have to make a very difficult choice? What feelings do you have after you've decided?
2. Can you think of an example where being honest is not a good idea?
3. How does lying to others hurt you?
4. How does doing the right thing, even when it's very tough, make you a better person?

Additional Sharing Circle Topics

I Had a Problem and Solved It

I Didn't Want to Have to Make a Decision

I Thought Over My Decision, and I Stuck to It

A Time I Used Good Judgment

I Thought It Over and Then Decided

Looking Back on a Decision I Made

I Had to Remake My Decision

What I Would Do If I Were an Adult

Something I Would Like to Achieve in the Next Three Years

Things I Can Do to Get Where I Want to Be

How I Earned Something and What I Did with It

I Put Off Making a Decision

A Decision I Lived to Regret

A Decision Someone Else Made That Affected Me

It Was My Decision, But Someone Else Made It

The Hardest Decision I've Ever Made

One of the Best Decisions I've Ever Made

I Made a Good Decision But Got a Poor Result

The Hardest Thing About Making Decisions Is...

The Easiest Thing About Making Decisions Is...

What It Takes to Be Decisive

A Time I Was Sure I Was Doing the Right Thing

I Time I Decided Based on My Feelings

A Time Someone Made an Unfair Decision

I Made a Decision and Regretted It Later

Managing Stress

Activities in this unit teach students to:

- identify feelings and bodily sensations associated with stress, and describe ways of handling stress.

- use deep breathing exercises to reduce and relieve stress.

- develop the habit of positive self-talk as a way of controlling stress-inducing thoughts and attitudes.

Sharing Circles in this unit allow students to:

- identify situations that cause them stress and discuss coping behaviors.

- describe resiliency behaviors that have helped them get through difficult situations.

Anatomy of Stress
Experience Sheet and Discussion

Objectives:

The students will:

—associate stressors with familiar physiological responses.

—describe actions they can take to relieve stress symptoms when they occur.

Materials:

one copy of the experience sheet, "Stress Alarm!" for each student

Procedure:

Engage the students in a discussion about stress and stressors. Explain that a stressor is any thought, condition, or event that causes a person to become anxious, worried, tense, or upset.

Point out that the human body has strong physiological reactions when confronted with a stressor. Ask the students to name some of the sensations they've noticed in their own bodies when they are tense or worried. List these on the board.

Distribute the experience sheets and read through the directions aloud. Instruct the students to complete the graphic outline of the body (on the sheet) by illustrating the various reactions listed. For example, suggest that they draw big worried eyes; a tight, panting mouth; a tummy full of butterflies; jittery hands; expanded lungs; and anything else they can think of. Encourage the students to use symbols and to be as creative as possible.

Have them form groups of six and share their completed drawings. Then display the drawings around the room. Lead a follow-up discussion.

Discussion Questions:

1. Why is it a good idea to know some of the reactions our bodies have to stress?
2. What are some things you can do to relieve these feelings when they occur?
3. What can you do if you start to feel anxious or worried, and are not sure why?

Stress Alarm!
Experience Sheet

When you get scared or think you have a big problem, your BRAIN sends out signals that prepare your body to fight or to run. Follow the path through the maze of body reactions.

First, a chemical called adrenaline speeds up your body system, and then...

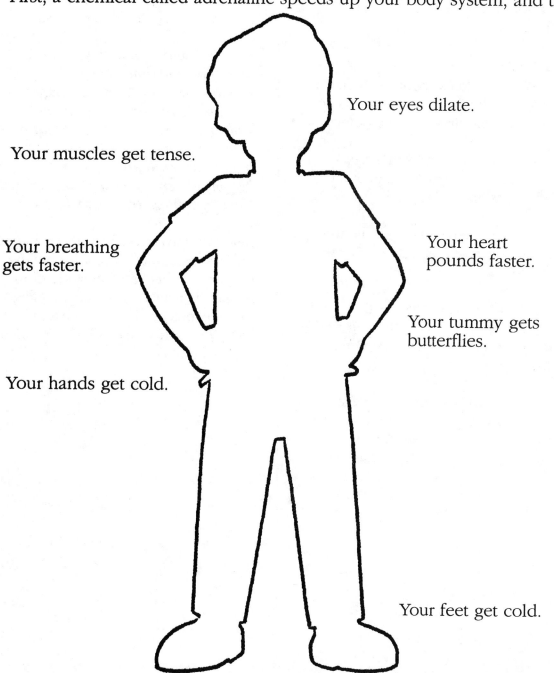

Your eyes dilate.

Your muscles get tense.

Your breathing gets faster.

Your heart pounds faster.

Your tummy gets butterflies.

Your hands get cold.

Your feet get cold.

Relaxation Breathing
Three Exercises with Coaching Tips

Objectives:
The students will:
—practice using deep breathing for relaxation and mental focus.
—discuss the health benefits of deep breathing.

Procedure:
Talk with your students about the benefits of deep breathing. Invite their comments and contributions while making these points:

• Deep breathing is relaxing. It eases tensions, anxiety, depression, irritability, muscular tension, and fatigue.

• Deep breathing helps to oxygenate the blood and improve feelings of general well-being.

• Shallow breathing, hyperventilation, cold hands and feet, and breath-holding can be prevented and treated with deep-breathing exercises.

• Deep breathing is a great way to ease stress during tense moments, such as prior to speaking in front of a group, taking a test, or dealing with a difficult situation.

Have students sit, stand, or lie in a quiet place. Sitting and standing posture should be erect, but relaxed — not rigid.

Before you begin the first exercise, in your own words, say to the students:

Pay close attention to how you are breathing, but don't worry if your mind wanders and you start thinking of homework, chores, television, or friends. Simply let those thoughts pass naturally and then return your attention to your breathing. Maintaining concentration will become easier and easier, and you will soon learn to control drifting thoughts.

After you have led an exercise at least once in class, distribute the corresponding experience sheet so that students may repeat the activity at home. Suggest that the students practice breathing exercises twice daily for approximately 5 to 10 minutes each session.

Natural Breathing
Experience Sheet

1. Sit up straight in a comfortable chair, or stand erect but relaxed.

2. Notice how you are breathing. Breathe slowly and deeply.

3. Close your eyes and breathe slowly through your nose. Inhale deeply so that the air fills the lower section of your lungs and your diaphragm pushes your stomach outward to make room for the air. Then, as your lower ribs and chest expand, fill the middle part of your lungs. Finally, as your chest rises slightly, fill the upper part of the lungs. Do this in one continuous motion as you inhale.

4. Hold the breath for a few seconds.

5. Exhale slowly through your nose and mouth. As you exhale, allow all of the tensions to leave your body.

6. Continue to breathe deeply like this for five minutes (or more).

7. Gently open your eyes. Stay seated (or standing) in the same position for a few moments.

8. Resume your normal schedule feeling more relaxed than before.

Windmill Breathing Exercise
Experience Sheet

1. Stand straight with your arms extended in front of you.

2. Inhale deeply so that the air fills the lower section of your lungs and your diaphragm pushes your stomach outward to make room for the air. Then, as your lower ribs and chest expand, fill the middle part of your lungs. Finally, as your chest rises slightly, fill the upper part of the lungs. Do this in one continuous motion as you inhale.

3. Rotate your arms backward in a circle several times.

4. Reverse direction and rotate your arms forward, or alternate directions like a windmill.

5. Exhale forcefully through your mouth.

6. Breathe several deep, purifying breaths.

Breathing and Visualization
Experience Sheet

Play relaxing music at a low volume (optional) while you read these directions:

Sit or lie in a comfortable position. Gently close your eyes and slowly breath in and out. Take a deep breath and let it out. (Pause.) Take another deep breath and let it go. (Pause.) Continue to breath deeply. Imagine a warm summer day. (Pause.) You are outside, lying on your back in lush green grass. You are looking at the sky, which is a beautiful blue. (Pause.) You see soft white fluffy clouds that look like large tufts of cotton. Point to one of the biggest clouds and, as you slowly pull your hand back, watch the cloud begin to drift toward you. (Pause.) See it float down close to the ground. Climb onto the cloud. Feel how soft and comfortable it is. As you breathe, feel the softness of the cloud and watch the cloud become pink. (Pause.) Take a deep breath and fill your lungs with the lovely pink of the cloud. (Pause.) Notice how you are feeling. (Pause.) Breathe in and out slowly. (Pause.) Now think of your favorite color and notice that your cloud has become that color. (Pause.) Take a deep breath and breathe in your favorite color. (Pause.) Notice how you are feeling now. (Pause.) Breathe in and out slowly. (Pause) Change the color again and notice how that color feels. (Pause.) Change the color one more time. (Pause.) Always notice how you feel. (Pause.) Now as you breathe out, watch all the colors flow out like a rainbow. Enjoy lying in your rainbow cloud. (Pause.) Say to yourself, "I am relaxed." "I feel good." "I am healthy." "The colors are pretty and relaxing." (Pause.) Take another deep breath and blow the beautiful rainbow cloud away. Watch your special cloud drift up and away. (Pause.) When you are ready, open your eyes and look around. Gently stretch and notice how relaxed and good you feel.

Self-Talk and Stress
Discussion and Game

Objectives:
The students will:

—state the importance of positive self-talk as an antidote to stress.

—describe the impact of self-talk on feelings and performance.

Materials:
index cards listing stressful situations (see directions, below)

Procedure:
Introduce this activity by discussing the connection between stress and self-talk. Invite input from the students while making these points and offering examples:

• Responses to stress come from within.
• Self-talk (the words we say to ourselves) serves as a major link between the things we believe about ourselves and our reactions to stress.
• We engage in self-talk during most of our waking moments.
• Self-talk is like a conversation we have with ourselves, often *about* ourselves.
• Whether we feel better or worse in stressful situations depends partly on what we say to ourselves.

To prepare for the game, think of a number of situations that commonly cause students to indulge in both positive and negative self-talk. Write the situations on index cards. (Use the situations listed below, add different situations based on your own observations, and ask the students to contribute others.)

Place the cards in a pile, face down.

Have a volunteer draw a card and read aloud the situation written on the card. Ask what the volunteer might say to himself or herself in that situation. For example, upon realizing that an important homework assignment has been left at home, a student might say, "I would forget my head if it weren't attached" or "The teacher's going to kill me."

Ask the class to decide if the statement represents negative or positive self-talk. You might call for a hand signal, such as "thumbs up" if the statement is positive or "thumbs down" if the statement is negative. If the statement is negative, give the student an opportunity to restate the response in positive terms. If the student has difficulty, ask the class to assist. For example, the student could say, "I forgot my homework today, but I am getting better at remembering my homework and other things. I have a good memory."

Continue until all of the cards have been drawn. Involve as many students as possible. Conduct a brief class discussion at the conclusion of the game.

Discussion Questions:
1. What differences did you notice between how you *felt* when your thoughts were positive and negative?
2. What do you find easiest about controlling self-talk? What do you find hardest?
3. What ideas do you have for getting control of your self-talk?

Situations:

- You forget to bring your homework to school.

- You get 4 out of 10 wrong on a spelling test.

- You get 9 out of 10 right on a quiz.

- You miss the school bus.

- You are left out of a game on the playground.

- You strike out in a softball game.

- You move to a new neighborhood.

- Your best friend goes shopping with someone else.

- You arrive late to class.

- You get an A on an assignment.

- A group project goes well.

- Your new haircut didn't turn out like you wanted it to.

- You spill your milk at lunch.

- You have a library book that is six weeks overdue.

- You run for student council and lose.

- You run for student council and win.

- Someone points out that you have a stain on your shirt.

- You have to complete a lengthy report on the civil war.

- You get a B- on your book report.

- You are asked to baby-sit.

Something That Causes Me Stress
A Sharing Circle

Objectives:

The students will:

—identify stressors in their lives.

—describe feelings and sensations associated with stress.

—name specific ways of dealing with stress.

Introduce the Topic.

Our topic for this session is, "Something That Causes Me Stress." Do you ever get tongue tied? Feel uptight or on edge? Get a headache or a queasy stomach when you're not sick? Chances are the cause of those feelings is stress. Many different things can cause stress — worrying about a test, feeling angry at someone, or not getting enough sleep, for example. Even good things can cause stress — like the excitement of waiting for a special event. Think of something that causes you stress and tell us about it. What happens to cause the stress, and how does it affect the way you feel, the thoughts you have, and the things you do? Take a few minutes to think about it. The topic is, "Something That Causes Me Stress."

Discussion Questions:

1. Do the same kinds of things frequently cause you stress?
2. If you know something is likely to stress you, what can you do about it?
3. Do feelings of stress do us any good? Explain your answer.

What I Do When the Going Gets Tough
A Sharing Circle

Objectives:
The students will:
—identify stressful experiences.
—describe positive ways of handling stress.

Introduce the Topic:
Our topic for this session is, "What I Do When the Going Gets Tough." Most of us have ways to make ourselves feel better when we are stressed. What's one of your ways? What do you do to help yourself when you feel angry, worried, tense, or nervous? Maybe you talk to one of your parents or to a friend about what's bothering you. Or perhaps you take a long walk or bike ride. Spending time alone with your pet may make you feel better. Or perhaps you do something to take your mind off the stressful situation — like watching TV, going to a movie, or reading a book. Tell us what you do, and how you feel when you do it. Let's think it over for a few moments. The topic is, "What I Do When the Going Gets Tough."

Discussion Questions:
1. How does your body feel when you are stressed?
2. Why is it important to find positive ways to handle stress?
3. What are some negative ways in which people try to handle stress?

Additional Sharing Circle Topics

I Was So Distressed I Got Sick

I Did Something for My Body and It Improved My Spirit

Something I Worried About That Turned Out Okay

A Time I Felt a Lot of Tension and Stress

Something I Do for My Own Well Being

I Problem I'm Trying to Solve

Someone I Can Talk to When I'm Worried

My Favorite Physical Exercise

Where I Go When I Want to Be Alone

A Way I Take Care of My Body

What I Say When I Talk to Myself

A Way I've Learned to Calm Myself Down

Music That Makes Me Feel Good

A Time I Felt Upset and Didn't Know Why

Self-concept

Activities in this unit teach students to:

- describe positive characteristics about themselves.

- recognize the importance of specific activities in which they participate and environments in which they live, and show how those contribute to their self-concept.

- give and accept positive feedback.

Sharing Circles in this unit allow students to:

- describe a deed or accomplishment from which they derive feelings of pride.

- identify a characteristic or trait in themselves that they accept and like.

Winning Qualities
Experience Sheet and Discussion in Triads

Objectives:

The children will:

—describe positive characteristics in themselves.

—demonstrate a positive attitude toward themselves.

—identify interests, abilities, and strengths as components of personal uniqueness.

Materials:

pencils for writing; one copy of the experience sheet, "Winning Qualities: Write a Sentence About Yourself!" for each child

Procedure:

Distribute the experience sheets. Read aloud the directions at the top of the experience sheet. Tell the students that they will have 10 minutes to complete the sheet. Explain that they will then have the opportunity to share their sentences with two classmates.

Have the students begin filling out the experience sheet. Circulate and lend assistance, as needed.

Have the students share their completed experience sheets in groups of three. Group students who are already seated near one another and who get along well. Tell the students to take turns reading their sentences. Allow about 2 minutes per child.

When the triad discussions are concluded, gather the group together and lead a culminating discussion.

Discussion Questions:

1. How does it feel to talk about yourself in this way to others?
2. Why is it good to say nice things about ourselves?
3. Why do you think it feels strange to complement yourself?

Winning Qualities: Write a Sentence about Yourself!
Experience Sheet

Here are three lists of words. On each list, check the words that describe you best, or write a word or two of your own on each list.

1. Adjective (pick 2)	**2. Noun (pick 1)**	**3. Action verb (pick 2)**
friendly	student	enjoys other people
polite	boy	learns quickly
honest	girl	works hard
dependable	person	is good at _____
cooperative	friend	achieves in school
creative		is great at _____
enthusiastic		gets along well with others
smart		is fun to be with
		has good ideas

Now, write a sentence that describes you. Write the words you checked in the blanks, as shown:

I am a _____ and _____ _____
         (from list 1)   (from list 1)   (from list 2)

who _____ and
                      (from list 3)

_____ .
                   (from list 3)

Images of Me
An Art Activity

Objectives:
The students will:
—graphically represent three different images of themselves.
—view and talk about the significance of each image and the feelings it engenders.

Materials:
Large shapes (circle, triangle, rectangle, etc.) cut from colored construction paper (at least three shapes per student); large sheets of white poster board or construction paper; colored markers, crayons, scissors, and glue

Procedure:
Introduce the concept of self-image. Explain that an image is a picture of something. It can be a photograph or drawing, and it can also be the image we see in our mind when we *think about* the real thing. Self-image is how we mentally see ourselves.

In your own words, explain further:

Each of us may has several different self-images. You may have one image when you think of yourself at home with your family, and a very different one when you think of yourself playing baseball with your friends. Today, I want you to think of three of the best images you have of yourself and draw them. Then, use those three drawings to design a poster all about you.

Give each student three different construction-paper shapes, and ask a couple of students to distribute scissors, markers/crayons, glue, and poster board. While the students are getting set up, write the following list on the board:

My Family and Me
Me and My Friends
A Favorite Place
A Favorite Possession
My Pet and Me
A Favorite Day of the Year
A Dream Vacation
A Favorite Game or Sport
My Best School Subject
Something I'm Proud Of

Read through the list with the students, and explain:

Choose any topic from the list, and write the topic at the top of one of your shapes. Draw a picture on that shape, showing the image you have of yourself when you think of that topic. Then, choose two more topics and illustrate those on your remaining two shapes. When you have illustrated all three shapes, move the shapes around on a sheet of poster board until you come up with a design that you like. Finally, glue the shapes in place. Title your poster, "Images of (your name)."

Circulate during the work phase of the activity, and engage the students in brief conversations about their pictures. When the posters are finished, one at a time have the students hold up their poster and briefly describe what is happening in each of the three pictures. Facilitate a culminating discussion about the importance of having positive self-images. Finally, display the posters around the room.

Discussion Questions:

1. When you imagine yourself in a positive picture, how do you feel?
2. When your image of yourself is poor, how do you feel?
3. Where do we get the images we have of ourselves?
4. Why is it important to see ourselves in positive ways?

Variations:

Provide several patterns, and have the students cut out their own shapes, or have them trace around the patterns to make the images directly on the poster board.

When working with young children, read through the list of topics several times. Then circulate and assist with labeling shapes and titling posters.

Strength Bombardment
A Game of Appreciation

Objectives:

The students will:

—become more aware of their own strengths and those of others.

—hear numerous positive statements about themselves.

—practice giving positive feedback.

Materials:

a small pad of self-sticking labels; one pencil and one large sheet of plain paper per student; chart paper and markers or chalkboard and chalk

Procedure:

Tell the students that today you are going to focus on strengths. Ask: *Do you know what a strength is?*

Discuss the concept briefly, explaining that all people have strengths - good qualities, talents, and skills that others like and that make them successful. Point out that there are many words which name strengths, and ask the students to help you list some of them. On the board or chart paper, develop a list that includes such things as:

nice	funny
handsome	good sport
generous	honest
kind	plays the piano well
runs fast	writes great stories
smart	good in Math
friendly	loyal
pretty hair	

Distribute the labels and pencils. Have the students label one sticker for each person in the class, writing the person's initials You should participate in this, too.

Instruct the students to go back through their stickers and write a positive statement on each one. Tell them to think about the person, look at the list of strengths on the board/chart, and describe a quality or ability that they like in that person. Allow plenty of time for this phase of the activity.

Give each student a plain piece of paper. Tell the students to write their name at the top. Then, gather the class in a single large circle and explain the strength bombardment exercise. In your own words, say:

One person at a time passes his or her sheet of paper around the circle. When the sheet comes to you, find the label you have made for that person and stick it on the sheet. Then look at the person, say his or her name, and describe the strength. You might say, "Ted, the strength I see in you is your humor." When it's your turn to receive strength statements, just listen and accept what people tell you. You may say "thank you," but that's all.

Proceed with the strength bombardment. Afterwards, lead a brief summary discussion. Suggest that the students take their strength papers home, display them on a wall or bulletin board, and look at them often.

Discussion Questions:

1. How did you feel when you were receiving strength statements?
2. How did you feel when you were giving strength statements'?
3. Why is it important to recognize our own strengths and those of others?

Something I Did (or Made) That I'm Proud Of
A Sharing Circle

Objectives:

The students will:

—acknowledge themselves for things they've accomplished.

—describe feelings and bodily sensations associated with being proud.

Introduce the Topic:

Our topic or this session is, "Something I Did (or Made) That I'm Proud Of." Think of something that you accomplished that you feel very good about. It can be something you did, like an assignment, chore, sports activity, or special event. Or it can be something you made, like a drawing, a model, a photograph, or a scrapbook.

Maybe you helped solve a problem for a friend or family member. Or perhaps you made great party invitations, or played with a younger brother or sister so your mom could do something she needed to do. Maybe you baked a batch of cookies without burning a single one. Or maybe you learned how to play your favorite song on the piano without making any mistakes. Whatever it was, you feel proud that you were able to do it. Take a moment or two to think of something. The topic is, "Something I Did (or Made) That I'm Proud Of."

Discussion Questions:

1. What kinds of things were we proud of?
2. What difference is there between being pleased and being proud?
3. What feelings and sensations do you have inside when you are proud?

Something I Like About Myself
A Sharing Circle

Objectives:

The students will:

—demonstrate a positive attitude about themselves.

—describe positive characteristics about themselves.

Introduce the Topic:

Today we are going to talk about something everybody loves to talk about. We will talk about ourselves — to say some very good and true things about ourselves. The topic is, "Something I Like About Myself."

Think about yourself for a few moments. You have so many good qualities that it may be hard to decide which one to talk about. Maybe you're glad to be yourself because you learn things so easily. Or maybe you are good at playing and having fun with your friends. Perhaps you like something about your body, like your curly hair or your freckles. Maybe you're proud of your ability to play games and sports well. Let's think about it for a moment. When you are ready to share, raise your hand. The topic is, "Something I Like About Myself."

Discussion Questions:

1. Why is it okay for us to say what we like about ourselves in the Sharing Circle?
2. Why is it good for us to take pride in ourselves?
3. How do other people let you know that they are proud of you?

Additional Sharing Circle Topics

What People Like About Me

Something I'm Good At

I Did Something That Made Me Feel Like a Good Person

When I Like Myself Most

Something I Accomplished That Really Pleased Me

A Time I Made a Big Effort and Succeeded

A Time I Knew I Could Do It

Something About Me That's Special

Something I Enjoy Doing Because It Gives Me a Feeling of Accomplishment

Something I Wish I Could Do Better

A Success I Recently Experienced

A Time I Won and Loved It

A Time I Lost and Took It Hard

First I Imagined It, Then I Created It

When Someone Expected the Very Best of Me

My Greatest Asset

Personal Responsibility

Activities in this unit teach students to:

- understand the meaning of responsible behavior by identifying the responsible actions of story characters.

- recognize what it means to seek excellence in particular endeavors, and describe some of the consequences of people behaving irresponsibly.

- learn and practice ways of resisting peer pressure.

Sharing Circles in this unit allow students to:

- describe incidents in which they kept their word, and discuss the relationship of trustworthiness to personal responsibility.

- identify at least one way in which they are responsible in their daily lives, and describe the benefits of responsible action.

What Is Responsibility?
Using Literature to Build a Definition

Objectives:

The students will:
—identify responsible characters in well known stories.
—define responsibility and describe responsible actions.

Materials:

classic, well-known literature selections that clearly illustrate responsibility on the part of one or more characters (*The Little Engine That Could, Horton Hatches the Who, The Wizard of Oz*); dictionary; art and writing materials; tagboard and magic markers; a banner that reads, "Responsible Action Is:"

Procedure:

Begin by telling the students that you have a challenge for them. Then write the word, *Responsibility* on the chalkboard, read it with the students, and talk about its meaning.

Listen to the response of each child who wishes to offer a definition, and then point out that the word itself gives an important clue. Ask the students, "Do you see two smaller words here?" Discuss the words, *response* and *ability*, and help the students recognize that responsibility means, literally, *the ability to respond or take action.*

Using the input of the students, write an initial definition on the chalkboard. Then, look up responsibility in the dictionary and see if the definition matches that which the students derived through discussion. Note key differences.

Use literature to provide examples of responsible actions. Read a story to the students, or read passages from a story with which they are already familiar. Then ask:
—*Who acted in a responsible way in this story?*
—*Was anyone not responsible (or irresponsible)?*
—*In what ways did (name of character) act responsibly?*
—*How would you feel if you were... (one of the children who would not get toys if the Little Engine was not so responsible?; the baby in the egg who would not hatch if Horton didn't keep it warm?; Dorothy and you didn't have the Scarecrow, Tin Woodsman, or Cowardly Lion to help you get to the Emerald City?)*
—*How do you feel about the characters who were irresponsible?*

Ask the students to think of a story they like in which a character demonstrates responsible action, and to draw a picture illustrating that character being responsible. Below their drawing, direct the students to write a sentence or paragraph describing the responsible action and how they feel about it. Circulate as the students draw and write, offering encouragement, acknowledgment, and assistance as needed.

Redirect the students to their initial definition of responsibility and ask them if they believe the definition can be improved. Facilitate further discussion about the meaning of responsibility, adding words to the definition, or writing a clarifying sentence or two on the board.

Write the revised definition on tagboard and post it at the top of a bulletin board under a banner reading, "Responsible Action Is:" Complete the display by posting the children's illustrations.

Discussion Questions:

1. Does responsible action just happen or do we do it on purpose? Explain.
2. Is an action responsible if it is sloppy or poorly done? Why or why not?
3. What do we need to do to be thought of as responsible people?

Striving for Excellence
Skits, Discussion, and Song

Objectives:

The students will:

—describe times when they did their best.

—creatively demonstrate what can happen when individuals don't do their best.

—explain the costs and benefits of pursuing excellence.

Materials:

chalkboard and chalk; copies of the song lyrics, "Who I Am Makes a Difference;" a simple tune for the song composed in advance; piano, guitar, or other musical instrument (optional)

Procedure:

Ask the students to think of a time when they did their very best at something — absolutely the most thorough, skillful, quality job they could do at the time. Tell them that this effort could have been made toward something very big and important or something relatively small. Emphasize that what you're after is the quality of the effort, not the importance of the end product. Suggest that the effort could have been made toward the accomplishment of things like:

• a school project
• a game or athletic event
• a single moment in an athletic event (like a particular time at bat)
• a household chore
• baking a cake or preparing a salad
• drawing a picture
• wrapping a present
• performing in a dance or music recital
• a spelling test or spelling bee

Invite several students to briefly share their incident with the class. Be sure to ask these volunteers how they felt about themselves for doing their best — and how other people felt about them. Introduce the concept of *excellence*, and talk about developing a habit of striving for excellence in every pursuit.

Write the following list on the board:

airline pilot
school bus driver
ball player
ballet dancer
fire fighter
doctor
architect or builder
baby-sitter
chef/cook
automobile mechanic
movie or TV actor
crossing guard

Have the students form groups of three or four. Announce that each group is going to develop a skit showing what can happen if one of the people listed on the board sloughs off and doesn't do his or her best.

Have each group select a recorder and choose a subject from the list (avoiding duplications). Suggest that the groups begin by describing a specific job that their subject might be doing, and then brainstorming possible consequences of the person's not doing his/her best. This process should give the groups plenty of material for a skit. Once their scenario is established, have them assign roles and rehearse.

One at a time, have the groups perform their completed skits for the entire class. After each skit, facilitate a brief discussion, focusing on the importance of doing one's best.

Conclude the activity by singing the song, "Who I Am Makes a Difference." Divide the class in half (groups 1 and 2). Play or hum the tune a couple of times. Then lead group 1 in singing the first chorus (A), pointing to group 2 when they sing the words, "and the same is true for you." Lead group 2 in singing the second chorus (B), with the students pointing back at group 1 on the last line. Have the entire class sing the last chorus (C) together. Finally, repeat the first chorus, signaling the children to point at each other as they speak the last line loudly and firmly.

Discussion Questions:

1. Who benefits when we do our best?
2. How do you know when you are doing your best?
3. What does it cost to do your best? What, if anything, do you have to give up?
4. Does striving for excellence build good character? How?

Who I Am Makes a Difference

A.
Who I am makes a difference,
What I do makes a difference,
What I say makes a difference, each and every day.
Who I am makes a difference,
What I do makes a difference,
What I say makes a difference, and the same is true for you.

B.
Who you are makes a difference,
What you do makes a difference,
What you say makes a difference, each and every day.
Who you are makes a difference,
What you do makes a difference,
What you say makes a difference, and the same is true for you.

C.
Who we are makes a difference,
What we do makes a difference,
What we say makes a difference, each and every day.
Who we are makes a difference,
What we do makes a difference
What we say makes a difference,
Yes, I know it's true.

Words and music copyright 1990 by Linda K. Williams

Recognizing Peer Pressure
Brainstorming and Discussion

Objectives:
The students will:
—describe peer pressure as an opportunity to exercise responsibility..
—identify types of peer pressure and their effects.

Materials:
chalkboard and chalk or chart paper and magic marker

Procedure:
Write the heading "Peer Pressure" on the chalkboard or chart paper. Gather the students together and, in your own words, define the term. For example, say: *A peer is someone who is like you in many ways. Your peers are about the same age as you are, they go to school like you do, and they like many of the same things that you like. The other children in this class are your peers. My peers are other adults who went to college and have jobs. For example, the principal and the other teachers in this school are my peers.*

Pressure is a type of force. For instance, when I push this door open, or close this drawer, I do it with the pressure of my hand (demonstrate). That's a type of physical *pressure. The kind of pressure we're going to talk about today, however, is not physical. Instead, it comes from the words and actions of other people.* Peer *pressure comes from the words and actions of your peers. If someone in this class tries to get you to do something that you don't want to do, that's an example of peer pressure. If your friend tries to get you to do something you* might *want to do,*

but aren't sure *about, that's peer pressure, too. Sometimes peer pressure is good, and sometimes it's harmful. Peer pressure is good when it makes us consider things that are good for us — like being friendly or playing fair. Peer pressure is harmful when it tries to get us to do something that is wrong or unhealthy.*

Write the following (or another) example on the board or chart:

• Billy is supposed to go to the library after school and pick out some books. Ted and Jeff try to convince him to play catch instead.

Discuss the example with the students. Use these and other open-ended questions:
—*Is this an example of good peer pressure or harmful peer sure?*
—*If Billy says no, and the other boys accept his answer, is it peer pressure?*
—*How do you think Billy feels when his friends try to get him to do something he's not supposed to do?*
—*What could happen if Billy gives in and plays catch instead of going to the library?*
—*What could happen if Billy refuses to play with his friends?*
—*What would you say if you were Billy? What would you do? What might happen if you said or did that?*

One at a time, list and discuss other examples of peer press. Use some of your own, ask the students to contribute some, or use the examples provided. Discuss each one with the children, asking open-ended questions (like those above) tailored to the example. When the students suggest ways of responding to a harmful pressure situation, write them down on the board/chart. Discuss how well each suggestion would work.

Peer-Pressure Situations:

• Mary wants to copy Angela's answers on a test.

• Dennis tries to get Bruce to get up earlier, so he won't be late for school.

• Molly wants Chris to ride his bike with her to the park on a other side of town, even though his parents told him not to ride that far.

• John wants David to smoke a cigarette.

• Judy tries to convince Michael to use hand signals when he rides his bike.

• Kelly urges Melinda to wear her mother's pearl necklace without permission.

• Paul tries to convince Tammy that school is boring and she shouldn't study so much.

• Jean and Lita think Janice is weird and urge Diane not to talk to her.

• Diane urges Jean and Lita to invite Janice to play with them.

• Joey tells Manny that boys shouldn't have teddy bears and urges Manny to throw his in the dumpster.

Conclude the activity. Emphasize that peer-pressure situations can take many forms, both good and harmful. It is important to recognize harmful peer pressure situations and know how to handle them.

A Time I Kept My Promise
A Sharing Circle

Objectives:

The students will:

—explain the value of keeping promises.

—associate feelings with honesty.

—associate honesty with the development of trust.

Introduce the Topic:

Today's topic is, "A Time I Kept My Promise." Have you ever made a promise to someone and kept it? You said that you were going to do something, or not do something, and you followed through — even though it might have taken some hard work. Maybe you promised your dad that you would sweep the kitchen or patio after school and you did it. Perhaps you made a promise to a friend that you would go to his house on a Saturday to help with math homework and you went, even though you had to give up a more enjoyable activity. Maybe you promised your teacher that you would try harder to be quiet during study time, and by really working at it you succeeded. Or perhaps you promised not to do something, like not to fight with your sister or brother when the two of you were alone. How did you feel about keeping your word? Did anyone notice or acknowledge you for keeping your promise? Try to remember a time that you made a promise and kept it, and get ready to share it with the group. The topic is, "A Time I Kept My Promise."

Discussion Questions:

1. Why is it important to keep promises when we make them?
2. How does it feel when someone makes a promise to you and keeps it? ...doesn't keep it?
3. How does keeping, or not keeping, promises affect the willingness of others to trust you?

A Way in Which I'm Responsible
A Sharing Circle

Objectives:

The students will:

—describe responsible behaviors in which they regularly engage.

—discuss the benefits of choosing responsible over irresponsble behaviors.

Introduce the Topic.

The topic for today's circle is, "A Way in Which I'm Responsible." Think of a responsibility that you accept and carry out. It may be a chore that you do each week, like sweeping the kitchen floor or watering the lawn. Perhaps your responsibility is to do your homework every evening after dinner, or to read for a half-hour each night before bed. Maybe you get up on time every morning, or fix breakfast for yourself and your younger brothers or sisters. Do you earn and save money? That is a way of being responsible. Before we begin, think quietly for a few moments about something you do that is responsible. The topic is, "A Way in Which I'm Responsible."

Discussion Questions:

1. What are some of the ways in which we are responsible?
2. What did you learn by hearing about what other students do that is responsible?
3. Why do you think it is important to be responsible?
4. What can happen when you are not a responsible person?

Additional Sharing Circle Topics

How I Help at School

How I Show That I'm a Good Citizen

How I Show Respect Toward Others

A Time I Helped Without Being Asked

A Promise That Was Hard to Keep

I Admitted That I Did It

I Stood Up for Something I Strongly Believe In

I Faced a Problem on My Own

I Told the Truth and Was Glad

I Kept an Agreement

A Responsible Habit I've Developed

A Time I Did Something to Help the Community

What I Wish I Could Do to Make This a Better World

People Seem to Respect Me When...

Someone Tried to Make Me Do Something I Didn't Want to Do

I Do My Best in School When...

A Time I Said "No" to Peer Pressure

A Way I Changed to Be a Better Friend

A Rule We Have in My Family

I Said Yes When I Wanted to Say No

A Time I Had the Courage of My Convictions

My Favorite Excuse

A Responsibility I Have at Home

A Time Someone Made a Promise to Me and Kept It

A Time I Didn't Keep My Promise

I Took a Positive Attitude Toward One of My Responsibilities

A Task I Didn't Like at First, But Do Like Now

An Irresponsible Habit I've Decided to Drop

A Responsible Habit I Plan to Have as an Adult

Empathy

Activities in this unit teach students to:

- identify nonverbal behaviors associated with various feelings by expressing those feelings in dramatizations.

- empathize with the feelings of another by consciously and deliberately taking that person's perspective.

- demonstrate empathy by reaching out and offering help and services to others.

Sharing Circles in this unit allow students to:

- identify times when they used good listening skills, and discuss how effective listening creates empathy.

- describe caring behaviors and discuss how expressions of caring benefit themselves and others.

Act Out a Feeling!
Dramatization and Discussion

Objectives:

The students will:

—identify feelings based on verbal and nonverbal cues.

—develop a working vocabulary for feeling words.

—state that feelings are natural and normal.

—describe the relationship between events and emotional reactions.

Materials:

at least 12 strips of plain paper; one black fine-tip marking pen; one empty can (coffee can size is perfect)

Procedure:

Tell the students that you have observed them displaying a lot of different feelings today, just as they do every day. Then describe a specific incident in which you were able to discern a person's feelings clearly. For example, describe how one person was hurt by the criticism or name-calling of another person. (Don't identify the individuals involved.) Ask the children if they noticed other incidents involving feelings, both positive and negative. Without naming names, discuss the various emotions demonstrated by people they (and you) observed.

As the students name feelings, write each feeling word down on a paper strip and put it in the can. After you have deposited a number of strips in the can, ask, "How can you tell by looking at a person how he or she feels?" After several responses, announce that the students are going to have an opportunity to act out the feelings they've been discussing.

Ask volunteers to come to the front of the room, draw a strip of paper from the can, and act out the feeling written on the paper. Emphasize that the students may express the feeling in any way they wish, using both body and face, but without naming the feeling. Explain that the rest of the class will try to guess what the feeling is. Give all volunteers an opportunity to participate.

Discussion Questions:

Between dramatizations, facilitate discussion. Each time a new feeling is dramatized, ask the class these questions:

1. What might cause a person to feel this way?
2. Can you remember a time when you had this feeling? In just a few words, tell us what happened.

After each of the emotions has been dramatized several times, conclude the activity with these questions:

1. What did you learn about feelings today?
2. Does everyone have the feelings we acted out? How do you know?
3. When you feel one of these feelings, or some other feeling, is it okay?
4. What do you feel inside when you *empathize* with another person's feelings?
5. When you feel angry or jealous, is it okay to do something that hurts another person? What can you do instead?

Reaching Out
Stories and Discussion

Objectives:
The students will:
—recognize and describe the feelings of others.
—demonstrate understanding of the needs of people who are different from themselves.
—recognize that all people, including those who are culturally and physically different from one another, share the same kinds of feelings.

Materials:
writing materials for older students; art materials for younger students

Procedure:
Choose one (or more) of the following stories and read it to the students. In your own words, say: *I'm going to read you a short story. I'd like you're help in thinking of some solutions to the problem that the person in the story is experiencing.*

After reading the story, facilitate a class discussion using the questions provided. Focus on helping your students identify and understand the feelings of the children in the story, *from their point of view.* Explain to the students that this kind of understanding is called *empathy* — the ability to "feel with" another person.

After the discussion, ask each student to write his or her own ending to the story (or to one of the stories, if you read several). If your students are very young, you may prefer to have them draw a picture illustrating a positive conclusion. Ask the students to share their story endings or illustrations with the class.

Jamil's First Day of School
Jamil entered his first-grade classroom as a non-English speaker, having just arrived from the Philippines. He had never been in a school before and, on his first day, he began running around the classroom making noises. When the teacher told him to sit down, he didn't understand what she said and continued to make silly humming sounds. The other children began to laugh and started to make noises, too. The teacher scolded the children, and said that they would have to give up 5 minutes of their recess to discuss their behavior. During the discussion, the teacher explained that Jamil did not understand English and never learned appropriate school behavior. She asked the children to help Jamil become a successful school citizen.

Discussion Questions:
1. How do you think Jamil felt being a new boy in the class?
2. How do you think Jamil felt not understanding what anyone said?
3. What could you do to help Jamil understand good school behavior?
4. What could Jamil have done to help the other children learn about his life in the Philippines?
5. How could you be Jamil's friend and help him learn English words?

Karla's Ordeal

Nine-year-old Karla tried to make friends at every school she attended, and this was the third school in the past year. But the other girls made fun of her old clothes and sometimes unbrushed hair and dirty face. Karla lived with her dad and two brothers in an old camper. They moved from one trailer park to another, in whatever town her father could find work. The camper had no running water, so Karla had to use the trailer-park bathrooms, which sometimes had neither showers nor hot water. At school, the children called her "Homeless Orphan" on the playground. "I am not homeless. I live in a trailer with my dad, who calls me his princess," Karla would answer. Finally, one of the older girls, overhearing the name-calling, shouted to the others, "Come on. Quit teasing Karla. She's the best artist in the school. I saw her pictures on the cafeteria bulletin board!"

Discussion Questions:

1. How do you think Karla felt when the other girls teased her?
2. Why do you think the older girl tried to defend Karla by shouting to the ones who were teasing her?
3. What could Karla have done to try to make friends with the girls who were teasing her?
4. What could the other girls have done to help Karla when she came to school with a dirty face?

Why Jerome Won't Talk

Jerome loved attending Scouts when they played outdoor games, made things out of wood or paper, or went hiking. He could run fast, catch balls, and make things with his hands better than most of the other boys. But when it came time to say the Scout promise or join in group discussions, Jerome wouldn't participate. Every time he tried to speak, he began to stutter, "I p-p-p-promise to d-d-do..." Jerome usually quit before he finished a sentence. Often, some of the boys put their hands over their mouths and giggled. Jerome saw this and he stopped even trying to speak. The Scout leader tried to encourage him to speak, "Come on, Jerome. Keep trying. It doesn't have to be perfect." But Jerome just looked down, silently.

Discussion Questions:

1. How do you think Jerome felt about stuttering when he talked?
2. How do you think Jerome felt when the boys giggled?
3. What could the boys have done to help him?
4. What could Jerome have done to make friends with the boys?

A Test of Friendship

Naomi and Lisa became good friends in the sixth grade. They were in the same class at school and lived in apartment buildings on the same city block. The girls took violin lessons together after school and played on the neighborhood soccer team. They often slept over at each other's apartments, and sometimes ate dinner with each other's families. The only problems the girls encountered in their friendship occurred on holidays, especially during the winter. Naomi was Jewish and celebrated holy days with her family, at home and in the synagogue. During Hanukkah in December, Naomi wanted to stay home with her family to light the candles on their menorah and play games with the dreidl. Lisa wanted Naomi to spend the night with her and decorate her family's Christmas tree. The girls had a big argument over this, which almost ruined their friendship.

Discussion Questions:

1. How do you think the girls could have solved their problem?
2. What could the girls' families have done to help them solve their problem?
3. How could the girls have used their differences to strengthen their friendship?

Dare to Care
Dramatizations

Objectives:

The students will:

—discuss ways of demonstrating empathy and caring.

—practice empathic, caring behaviors in a variety of dramatized scenarios.

Materials:

chalkboard or whiteboard and writing implement; found materials for props (optional)

Procedure:

Explain to the students that there are many ways to demonstrate empathy and caring. Ask the students to think about ways in which they can show care and concern for other people. Generate a list of words and phrases that describe ways of caring and write them on the board. Here are some suggestions:

- listening
- cheering up someone
- helping
- volunteering
- inviting
- sharing
- smiling
- patting
- acknowledging
- thanking
- greeting new students
- accompanying
- hugging
- shaking hands
- thinking about your actions and their consequences
- treating others fairly
- giving presents
- singing to someone
- writing to a friend.

Discuss possible role-play situations using one of the words or phrases on the list. For example, the word volunteering could generate these scenarios:

A teacher introduces a new student and asks if someone would show her around the school and help her set up her desk during the next recess. A student raises his hand to volunteer and does the job.

A child, noticing that mom is very tired from working all day, volunteers to set the table for dinner and clear the table afterwards.

Discuss the possible actions and dialogue that might take place in each scenario. Then model the role-playing process by choosing volunteers to act out each scenario.

Divide the class into small groups and have each group choose one of the words from the board. Tell the groups to develop two or three scenarios that, when acted out, will effectively demonstrate that caring behavior. Have them assign a group member to each role, and then practice the scenario, making sure that every person has at least one part to play. Ask the students to repeat this procedure for each scenario they develop.

When the groups are finished practicing, invite them to dramatize their scenarios for the rest of the class. After each group is finished, discuss that group's dramatizations before going on to the next group. Ask, "How did these situations demonstrate the value of caring?"

Following all of the dramatizations, facilitate a culminating discussion.

Discussion Questions:

1. How do you know how another person feels?
2. Did feeling empathy for the other person in your scenario help you decide how to show caring?
3. What is empathy and how do you know when you've got it?
4. How do you know when a behavior shows caring?
5. What would life be like if no one cared about you? ...if you cared about no one?
6. Is it possible to care about people we don't know? Explain.

A Time I Listened Well to Someone
A Sharing Circle

Objectives:

The students will:

—recall incidents in which they demonstrated good listening skills.

—recognize the relationship between listening and empathy.

Introduce the Topic:

Most of us appreciate having someone really listen to us. Listening is one of the most best ways of understanding and feeling empathy for other people. In this session we are going to turn this idea around and talk about how it feels to listen to and empathize with someone else. The topic is, "A Time I Listened Well to Someone."

Can you remember a time when you really paid attention to someone and listened carefully to what he or she said? This means that you didn't interrupt with your own ideas or daydream about your own plans, but really concentrated and tried to understand what the other person was feeling and attempting to get across. Maybe you've listened to a friend like that, or a younger brother or sister, or a teacher or coach. Think about it for a few moments and, if you wish, tell us about, "A Time I Listened Well to Someone."

Discussion Questions:

1. What kinds of things make listening difficult?
2. Why is listening so important
2. Why is it important to listen to others?
3. What could you do to improve your listening?
4. How do you feel when someone really listens to you?

A Time I Showed Someone That I Cared
A Sharing Circle

Objectives:

The students will:

—recall incidents in which they showed caring, empathic behavior.

—acknowledge, validate, and support the caring behaviors of others.

Introduce the Topic:

Our topic today is, "A Time I Showed Someone That I Cared." We are all affected by people who care about us. And we have the ability to influence how others feel as well. Think of a time when you showed someone that you empathized and cared and it made the person feel good. Have you ever tried to cheer up a friend who was feeling badly? Perhaps you helped a younger brother with his homework or a little sister tie her shoes. Maybe when your parent was tired from working all day, you helped prepare dinner. Or maybe you told a friend that you understood how he or she felt because you'd felt that same way. How did the person react to your empathy and caring behavior? How did you feel about what you did? Think of the many times you have shown someone that you cared, and share one example with us. Our topic is, "A Time I Showed Someone That I Cared."

Discussion Questions:

1. How do we affect the world we live in when we show people that we understand and care about them?
2. Why is it important for us to see ourselves as caring people?
3. How do we learn to be caring people? How do we learn empathy?

Additional Sharing Circle Topics

A Time When I Accepted Someone Else's Feelings
Someone Didn't Say a Word, But I Knew How S/he Felt
I Didn't Say a Word, But They Knew How I Felt
A Time I Put Myself in Someone Else's Shoes
A Time I Felt Sorry for Someone Who Was Put Down
I Helped Someone Who Needed and Wanted My Help
A Time I Listened Well to Someone
Someone Who Always Understands Me
A Person I Can Share My Feelings With
How I Show That I Care
A Time I Could Have Shown That I Cared, But Didn't
A Time I Failed to Listen to Someone
A Time Someone Really Listened to Me
A Time Someone Failed to Listen to Me
One of the Most Caring People I Know
A Time Someone Understood My Point of View
A Time My Point of View Was Misunderstood

Communication

Activities in this unit teach students to:

- associate nonverbal communication behaviors with particular feelings.

- listen accurately and carefully.

- engage in effective two-way communication, using good listening and speaking skills.

Sharing Circles in this unit allow students to:

- explore the importance of listening and discuss how they feel when someone refuses to listen to them.

- describe ways of getting the attention of another person as a prelude to expressing themselves, and distinguish between positive, effective, and negative, ineffective, methods of getting attention.

Let Your Feelings Be Your Guide!
Movement/Observation Activity

Objectives:
The students will:
—demonstrate appropriate nonverbal behaviors.
—practice reading the nonverbal behaviors of others.

Materials:
A list of situations, each of which generates a different emotion or reaction. For example, "Your teacher just caught you looking on someone else's test paper;" "Your mom just said you can have a puppy;" "You just ruined your favorite CD or tape;" "You are home alone and you hear strange noises outside your bedroom window;" "Your little sister or brother has been fooling around in your room;" "You have just been given a good citizenship award from the school principal"

Procedure:
Ask the students to form a circle. Have them extend their arms outward and touch each other's outstretched hands. This will allow plenty of space for movement.

Explain: *When I call out a situation, you must respond nonverbally in a way that seems appropriate to that situation. For example, if I say, "You have just won the lottery," you might do this: (Demonstrate by jumping up and down, waving your arms, or letting your mouth drop open). Now show me how you would respond to the lottery example. While you are reacting, notice the reactions of others too.*

Encourage the students to really get into it.

Call out another situation such as, "Your best friend just moved to another city." Allow enough time for the students to respond. Remind them to respond nonverbally, and to look around and make mental note of the different ways in which the other children respond.

Continue calling out situations until you have exhausted your list.

Discussion Questions:
1. What kinds of actions or gestures were used for positive reactions? ...for negative reactions?
2. Can you recall seeing someone react differently than you did to the same situation?
3. What did you notice about people's facial expressions?
4. Why is noticing nonverbal behavior such an important part of communication?

Play Back!
Preliminary Listening Exercise

Objectives:
The students will:
—demonstrate careful listening.
—describe the importance of good listening to friendships, family, and relationships.

Materials:
audiocassette recorder and blank tape

Procedure:
Preparation: While the students are working, inconspicuously move around the room and tape some of their comments and casual conversation. Try to get clear recordings of individual student's voices that will be easily recognized.

Begin playing the recorded sounds at a relatively low volume, and then gather the students together. Write "Listen!" on the chalkboard in large letters. Point to the word and use other nonverbal signals to get the students to obey the written command. Let them listen to the sound of the tape recorder for a few moments, and then turn it off. Ask the students what they think they heard. Accept their responses, and then suggest that the tape recorder was "listening" to them while they worked. Ask the students, "What is special about the way a tape recorder listens?"

Facilitate responses to the question, helping the students recognize that a tape recorder is usually very accurate. If it is working properly, a tape recorder hears every word just the way it is said. In your own words

say to the students: *You and a partner are going to take turns pretending to be tape recorders. When you are a tape recorder, you must listen very carefully to every word your partner says. Then, when your partner asks you to "play back" your recording, you will be able to repeat — just like a tape recorder — the things your partner told you.*

Have the students choose partners. Ask them to decide who will play the part of the tape recorder first. Have the "tape recorders" raise their hands. Explain that the other students will talk first, and that you will call time after 1 minute. Announce this topic:

"What I'm Going To Do After School Today"

Tell the speakers to start talking and the "tape recorders" to start recording. Call time after 1 minute. Give the next instruction: *Now the "tape recorders" will have 1 minute to repeat what they heard, while the speakers listen.*

Call time after 1 minute and ask the students these questions:
—*What was it like to listen like a tape recorder?*
—*Speakers, how well did your tape recorder work?*
—*What was it like to be listened to so well?*

Have the students switch roles and repeat the entire process, using the same topic. Then, ask the students to find new partners. Lead another round of the activity (with both partners having a turn) using this topic:

"What I'd Like To Do on My Birthday"

As time and interest permit, conduct additional rounds, switching partners and topics with each new round. Lead a follow-up discussion, focusing on the importance of listening.

Discussion Questions:

1. Why is it important to listen carefully when someone is talking?
2. How do you feel when someone listens to you and tries to understand everything you say?
3. How do you feel when the person you are talking to doesn't listen?
4. Why is it important to listen to your parents? ...your teacher? ...your friends?
5. Can good listening help people solve problems and conflicts that they have with each other? How?

Communication Counts!
Sending and Receiving Messages

Objectives:
The students will:
—define communication and identify ways in which people communicate.
—state rules for effective listening and speaking.
—demonstrate good listening and speaking in a practice session.

Materials:
chalkboard and chalk

Procedure:
Write the word *communication* on the chalkboard. Explain to the students that communication is a word that describes the way people send and receive messages. Ask the students to think of ways in which people communicate with each other. (talking face-to-face, telephone, writing, computer, television, radio, sign language, body language, etc.)

Ask two volunteers to come to the front of class. Tell them to say something to each other. Point out that during verbal communication between two people, there is always a listener and a speaker. When one person speaks, the other listens. Usually both people take turns in both roles. Tell the students that good communicators know how to listen well, and they also know how to speak well. These are skills that anyone can learn.

Ask the students to help you generate a list of rules for good listening. Suggest that they think of someone who listens well to them, and describe the things that person does. Write their ideas on the chalkboard, making sure that the list includes these items:
• Look at the speaker.
• Think about, or picture, what the speaker is saying.
• Don't interrupt.
• Show the speaker that you are listening by nodding, smiling, or making brief comments like, "That's neat" or "Sounds like fun" or "That's too bad." If you don't understand something the speaker says, ask a question.

Now, ask the students to help you generate a list of rules for good speaking. Suggest that they think of someone they know who speaks well and describe what that person does. Write their ideas on the chalkboard, making sure that the list includes these items:

• Think about what you want to say before you speak.
• Speak clearly and loud enough to be heard, but don't shout.
• Share the time equally with the other person.
• Don't change the subject unless it's okay with the other person.

List some topics on the board that the students can use during a practice session. For example:

1. A school rule you appreciate and how it helps you.
2. A school rule you don't like, and how you'd change it.
3. The importance of complimenting others, and why it feels good to get a compliment.
4. Other methods of communicating that you use, such as writing and receiving letters.
5. Your pet and how you train and care for it.

Have the students pair up and sit together. Ask them to decide who is **A** and who is **B**. Announce that the **A**'s will start the first conversation, using the topic of their choice. Tell the **B**'s to join in the conversation, being a good listener at first, and a good speaker every time it is their turn to talk. Review the rules for both listening and speaking.

Allow the partners to talk for 2 to 4 minutes, depending on their level of interest. Then ask the **B**'s to start a new conversation, using a different topic. Review the procedure and the rules as necessary. In a follow-up discussion ask questions to encourage the students to talk about the experience:

Discussion Questions:

1. Which rules for good listening were easiest to follow? ... hardest to follow?
2. Which rules for good speaking were easiest to follow? ... hardest to follow?
3. Which rules, if any, don't you understand?
4. How did you feel when you were listening?
5. How did you feel when you were speaking.
6. How do you feel when someone listens well to you?
7. How can being a good listener help you in school? ... in your friendships? ... in your family?
8. How can being a good speaker help you?

Once When Someone Wouldn't Listen to Me
A Sharing Circle

Objectives:

The students will:

—relate an example of failed communication caused by poor listening.

—discuss the importance of listening to good communication.

Introduce the Topic:

Today we are going to talk about one of the frustrations that occurs in the communication process. The topic is, "Once When Someone Wouldn't Listen to Me."

Have you ever tried to get someone to listen to you, and failed? Tell us about it. Maybe you came home wanting to relate an exciting experience to your family and no one would stop long enough to listen. Perhaps you had a question while shopping, but the sales person ignored you. Or maybe you were dealing with a particularly troubling problem and tried to discuss it with a friend, but he or she kept changing the subject or getting distracted. Take a minute to think about it, and tell us about a time when you had an experience like this. The topic is, "Once When Someone Wouldn't Listen to Me."

Discussion Questions:

1. What similarities and differences did you notice in our feelings about not being listened to?
2. How can you handle situations in which you aren't being listened to?
3. What have you learned from this discussion about listening to others?

How I Get People to Pay Attention to Me
A Sharing Circle

Objectives:

The students will:

—explore methods of capturing the attention of others.

—describe feelings generated by attention and lack of attention.

Introduce the Topic:

Today our topic is, "How I Get People to Pay Attention to Me." When you or I want to communicate with someone, first of all we have to get that person to focus on us. There are many ways to do this. For example, if you do something funny, destructive, or bizarre, people will automatically look at you. If you don't want every head in the room to turn, you have to do something less unusual. What do you do?

How do you get the attention of a family member engrossed in a TV program? What do you do to get the attention of a friend some distance from you in a large crowd? How do you capture the attention of someone two tables away in a quiet classroom or library? If you can think of a specific incident in which you used a particular method, tell us about it. The topic is, "How I Get People to Pay Attention to Me."

Discussion Questions:

1. When do we need to capture the attention of others?
2. What relationship is there between the way you get attention, the kind of attention you get, and how long the attention lasts?
3. How do you feel when a person refuses to pay attention to you no matter what you do?
4. Why do we need attention from others?

Additional Sharing Circle Topics

What I Think Good Communication Is

When What Was Said Was Not What Was Meant

A Time When Listening Would Have Kept Me Out of Trouble

I Told Someone How I Was Feeling

A Time I Listened Well to Someone

Something I See Differently Than My Parents See It

How I Used Sharing Circle Skills Outside the Circle

A Time I Said One Thing But Meant Another

A Time When I Communicated Well

What I Do to Make Myself Understood

A Time When Poor Communication Caused a Misunderstanding

What I Think Poor Communication Is

Group Dynamics

Activities in this unit teach students to:

- recognize the benefits of working together cooperatively.

- make a group decision, evaluate their behaviors in the group and identify successful strategies used to resolve disagreements.

- assess their strengths and weaknesses as team members.

Sharing Circles in this unit allow students to:

- identify and qualities of a group to which they enjoy belonging.

- describe an accomplishment produced and shared with other members of a group or team.

Working Together
Discussion and Experience Sheet

Objectives:
The students will:
—define the word *cooperate*.
—describe the benefits of cooperating with others to achieve a goal.

Materials:
one copy of the experience sheet, "Together Is Better" for each student; chalkboard and chalk

Procedure:
Write the word *cooperate* on the board. Ask the students what it means to cooperate with another person. Accept all contributions, jotting key words and phrases on the board. Attempt to agree upon a simple definition of the word.

Remind he students of specific occasions when you have asked groups of two or more to work together to complete a task or assignment. Ask them to think carefully about what they accomplished and how they went about it. Then ask, "What did you gain by working together cooperatively?"

Again, accept all contributions. Through questions and discussion, help the students identify the following potential benefits of working cooperatively with another person:
• When people work together, they save time.
• When people work together, they think of more solutions to a problem.
• When people work together, their solutions are more creative.
• When people work together, they have fun.
• When people work together, they do a better job.

Distribute the experience sheets. After going over the directions, give the students a few minutes to complete the sheet. If time permits, have the students share what they have written in small groups. Facilitate a culminating class discussion.

Discussion Questions:
1. What are some ways that you cooperate with others at home?
2. Why is it important to cooperate when working with others?
3. What happens when one person in a group is uncooperative?
4. If you had an uncooperative person in your group, what could you do?

Together Is Better
Experience Sheet

In the space below, write two or three sentences that describe what cooperating means to you. Below are some words that you might want to use. Use other words, too.

share   work
compromise   laugh
help   listen
team   enjoy
win   accomplish
think   talk
together   support

Cooperating means... _____

_____

_____

_____

_____

_____

_____

_____

Now use the back of this paper, and write about a time when you cooperated with someone to accomplish a goal, instead of working alone.

Donor Dollars
A Group Decision-Making Activity

Objectives:

The students will:

—experience group conflict caused by opposing opinions and beliefs.

—use communication and negotiation skills to reach a group decision.

Materials:

one copy of the list of choices for each small group; chalkboard and chalk

Procedure:

Have the students form small groups of four to six. Announce that the members of each group are going to work together to make a decision. In your own words, elaborate:

I want you to pretend that you are the student council for our school. This is an exciting time for you because you have an important decision to make. The council has been given $10,000 by an anonymous donor, which you must decide how to spend. However, the donor has narrowed your range of choices. You must decide from among six alternatives.

Give each group a copy of the list of choices. Read through the list with the students:

1. Take the student council (your group) to Disney World.

2. Use the money to purchase all new playground equipment.

3. Host a big party for the entire school.

4. Donate the money to a homeless shelter.

5. Fund badly needed remodeling at a nearby senior center in exchange for a plaque bearing every student's name.

6. Give every teacher at your school a cash bonus.

Explain to the students that they will have 20 minutes to reach a decision. List the following rules for interaction on the board and discuss as needed:

• One person speaks at a time, with no interruptions.

• Listen to and consider the ideas and opinions of all members.

• Consider the benefits and drawbacks of each alternative.

• Agree on one choice that is acceptable to all members of the group.

After calling time, give the groups an additional 5 minutes to discuss their behavior during the decision-making process. Then gather the entire group together for a culminating discussion.

Discussion Questions

1. What kind of communication took place in your group?
2. What were the major disagreements or conflicts in your group?
3. What conflict management skills were used to resolve disagreements?
4. Did anyone take the role of mediator in your group? If so, how was that done?
5. What did you learn about group decision making from this activity?

Cooperating With Others
Self-Assessment and Group Task

Objectives:

The students will:

—assess their attitudes and behaviors in group situations.

—describe the qualities and abilities they bring to groups.

—list the most important qualities of a group member.

Materials:

one copy of the self-assessment, "The Group and I," for each student; writing materials; several samples of want ads (optional)

Procedure:

Distribute the self-assessments. Explain that you want the students to take a few minutes to evaluate the attitudes and behaviors they have in groups. Answer any questions about procedure and then give the students 5 to 10 minutes to complete the assessment. When the students are finished, assure them that the contents of their self-assessments are private. Ask them to take a few moments to review what they have written, and then fold the sheets over or put them away.

Have the students form groups of four to six. Ask them to think of one thing that they learned from completing the self-assessment that they wouldn't mind sharing with their group. Allow about 15 minutes for sharing.

When they have finished sharing, tell the groups that you want them to work together to write a "want ad" for a qualified group member. (If you have ad samples, give one to each group.) Tell the groups to list in their ad the most important qualifications a group member should have. Explain that the qualities and abilities they list should be of benefit to almost any kind of group. (If you are working with very young students, facilitate this portion of the activity with the total group.)

When the groups have finished, ask them to share their ads with the rest of the class. Facilitate a class discussion.

Discussion Question:

1. What are the most important qualities/ abilities a person can bring to a group? Why are they so important?
2. How can a group bring out the best in each of its members?
3. Do members of a group always have to agree? Why or why not?
4. What can you do when disagreements and conflict erupt in a group?

The Group and I
Self-Assessment

How do you feel about cooperating with others? What are your actions?
Read each set of statements. Put an **X** on the line to show how you rate yourself.

I usually avoid group activities.	I take part in group activities as often as possible.
I'm never the first person to start a conversation.	I go out of my way to start conversations with other people.
I prefer to be alone.	I try to be with other people.
When I'm in a group, I don't say much.	I contribute a lot to every group I'm with.
I am not an important group member.	My membership in a group is always important.

Think of a time when you helped a group accomplish its goal. List the three most important qualities or abilities you brought to the group.

1._____

2._____

3._____

A Group I Like Belonging To
A Sharing Circle

Objectives:

The students will:

—describe benefits of belonging to a group.

—identify qualities of successful groups.

Introduce the Topic:

Today our topic is, "A Group I Like Belonging To." One of the most important things in life for most of us is being part of a group of people whom we enjoy and with whom we share common interests or goals. So today we are going to talk about groups we belong to and how it feels to belong.

If you decide to share, tell about a group you belong to. It could be a club or organization here at school, at church, or somewhere else. Or it could be a group of friends who get together frequently. Tell about one thing the group does that you enjoy, how you contribute to it, what the group contributes to you, and how you feel about belonging. Today's topic is, "A Group I Like Belonging To."

Discussion Questions:

1. Why do people join groups, clubs, or organizations?
2. What things did we most like about the groups we described?
3. What are some of the problems that groups often have?

We Worked Together to Get It Done
A Sharing Circle

Objectives:

The students will:

—describe the importance of cooperation in accomplishing a task.

—state some of the benefits of working with others.

Introduce the Topic:

Our topic for today is, "We Worked Together to Get It Done." Many times we do things all by ourselves, but sometimes it is necessary or more fun to do things with other people. Think of a time when you did something with others. Perhaps you and a friend, or you and your family, worked together to finish something — like a Halloween costume, or a holiday dinner. Maybe you and your Mom did the dishes together, or you and a friend put together a puzzle. Have you and a brother or sister ever worked together to make cookies, or build a sand castle? Think about it for a minute or two, and when you are ready to share, please raise your hand. The topic is, "We Worked Together to Get It Done."

Discussion Questions:

1. Do you think it is easier to get the job done with other people helping?

2. How did you decide who was going to do what?

3. If you were going to do the same job again, would you do the part of the job that you did this time, or would you do a different part of the job? Which part?

Additional Sharing Circle Topics

A Time I Felt Left Out
A Time I Worked in a Successful Group
We Cooperated to Get It Done
A Skill or Talent I Brought to the Team
A Time I Let the Team Down
A Role I Play in Groups
My Favorite Team
Something I Did That Helped the Team Succeed
A Way I Show Respect for Others
We Compromised to Get It Done
When the Easy Way Out Made Things Worse
A Time I Didn't Want to Be a Member of a Group
A Time I Felt Included
I Went Out of My Way to Include Someone Else
What I Think Makes a Winning Team
I Contributed Something Important to the Group

Conflict Resolution

Activities in this unit teach students to:

- define four distinct types of conflict, research real examples of each, and develop a vocabulary list of conflict-related terms.

- distinguish between three distinct reactions to typical conflict situations — denial, negative confrontation, and problem solving — and discuss the probable consequences of each.

- learn and practice eight conflict resolution strategies.

Sharing Circles in this unit allow students to:

- recognize how feelings and moods generated by one incident can be transferred to and affect the outcome of subsequent situations.

- examine avoidance behavior based on fear of conflict and discuss the consequences of avoiding conflict in specific situations.

What Is Conflict?
Illustrations, Categorizing, Vocabulary and Discussion

Objectives:

The students will:

—learn and practice vocabulary related to conflict.

—identify and discuss four major conflict categories.

—explain that people perceive conflict differently.

—describe the effects of conflict-related versus peaceful vocabulary.

—apply knowledge of four types of conflict to real-life situations.

Materials:

markers, blank paper, tape, and one copy of the experience sheet, "Conflict Clipping" for each student

Procedure:

Begin by having the students draw a picture that depicts conflict to them. Tell them to draw anything that comes to mind when they think about conflict. When the drawings are complete, post them around the room.

Ask the students to look closely at the drawings. If they need to get up and walk around, allow a few minutes to accomplish this. Then, ask the students to describe in their own words the different types of conflict shown. Ask: "Are there any conflicts in these drawings that seem to go together?"

Facilitate a sharing of insights and observations. Then, ask the students to physically group their drawings into four major conflict categories:

- **Intrapersonal:** conflict within an individual
- **Interpersonal:** conflict between two or more individuals
- **Intergroup:** conflict between organizations or groups of people
- **International:** conflict between nations or countries

Define and discuss the types of conflict. Ask the students to generate additional examples in each category.

Distribute the experience sheet, "Conflict Clipping," and explain the homework assignment. In your own words, say:

Your assignment is to find a newspaper article, cartoon, or photograph depicting a conflict. Read the article and answer the questions on the experience sheet. Bring both the clipping and the experience sheet to our next session. (Younger students will need help from their family.)

At the next session, ask the students to take out their homework assignment. Each student should have completed the experience sheet and brought in a clipped current-events article, photograph, or cartoon illustrating a conflict situation.

Have the students take turns summarizing their articles and sharing their responses on the experience sheet. The following questions may help focus the discussion:

—*Which type of conflict (of the four major types) is illustrated by your clipping?*

—*Which type of conflict seems to be most common? Why do you think that is?*

—*Does anyone want to guess how the conflict in their clipping will be resolved?*

Ask the students to brainstorm all the words they can that are related to conflict. On chart paper, make separate lists of verbs, nouns, and adjectives and post them around the room. Facilitate a culminating discussion.

Discussion Questions:

1. What kind of conflict are you having when you can't decide between two things that you want to buy?
2. When one nation sends troops to attack another nation, what kind of conflict is that?
3. Can you think of any intergroup conflicts that occur in our cities? ... our nation?
4. Can you think of an international conflict that is happening right now or happened recently?
5. Why is it important to know what words are often associated with conflict?
6. If someone approaches you and starts using a lot of conflict words, how do you feel? If someone says a lot of conflict words to you, what might happen if you use peaceful words to respond?
8. How can this information help you manage conflict?

Conflict Clipping
Experience Sheet

Look in a recent newspaper or magazine, and find a current events article, photograph, or cartoon about some kind of conflict. Cut it out. Answer the questions below. Bring this sheet and the clipping to the next session.

1. What is this conflict about?_____

_____

_____

_____

2. What type of conflict is it? Circle one:

      Intrapersonal   Interpersonal   Intergroup   International

3. Who is involved in the conflict?_____

_____

_____

_____

4. What does each person (or group, or nation) want?_____

_____

_____

_____

5. What do you think will happen?_____

_____

_____

_____

One Conflict with Three Endings
Story and Discussion

Objectives:

The students will:

—distinguish between denial, confrontation, and problem solving as responses to conflict.

—explain why problem solving is preferable to denial and confrontation.

Materials:

writing materials for the variation (see next page)

Procedure:

Read the following story to the students three times — first with Ending 1, then with Ending 2, and finally with Ending 3. Dramatize the dialogue to underscore differences between the three approaches.

Arturo and David are building a model with LEGOs. Mike comes over and asks if he can join in.

Ending 1:

Arturo says, "Sure." David doesn't like Mike very much and would rather that he didn't join them. Instead of saying anything, he just shrugs his shoulders and keeps working. Whenever Mike makes a suggestion, David says it's "dumb." And two or three times he grabs parts from Mike without asking. After a few minutes of this, Mike asks him what's bugging him. He sighs and says, "Nothing."

Ending 2:

Arturo says, "Sure," but David says, "No way!" Mike asks, "Why not?" David responds, "I hate working with you. You always act like you know everything. You don't listen, and you think your ideas are better than everyone else's." Mike shouts, "You're a liar. You're just jealous because I'm smarter than you are!" David is mad now and says, "You'd better get out of here before I make you!" Mike says, "On yeah? Try it." David moves around the table toward Mike, who runs to the other side of the room.

Ending 3:

Arturo says, "Sure," but David says, "No way!" Arturo asks, "Why don't you want him to work with us?" David responds, "Because I hate working with him. He always acts like he knows everything. He thinks his ideas are better than everyone else's." Mike points out to Arturo that he and David have been using the LEGOs for a long time, and that they really belong to the class, not just to the two of them. Arturo agrees with Mike and offers to let Mike work with him on the part of the model that he is building. David says, "I guess that's okay, if you promise to listen to my ideas, too." Mike answers, "Sure, I'll listen to you. And I'll work on this side of the model with Arturo. But if I have a suggestion about your part, can I ask you if it's okay to make it?" David grins. "Sure," he says.

Ask the students to describe the differences between the three endings. If necessary, read the endings again and discuss one at a time. Explaining the meaning of new words/concepts, help the students see these differences:

- In the first ending, David pretends there is no conflict. He is passive.
- In the second ending, David is using confrontation to respond to the conflict. Both he and Mike are being aggressive.
- In the third ending, all three boys are using problem solving to resolve the conflict. They are being assertive.

Discuss the differences between denial (pretending nothing's wrong), physical confrontation (fighting), and problem solving. Then read additional story starters and ask the class to help you make up three endings to each one — the first using denial, the second using negative confrontation, and the third using problem solving. Encourage the students to imagine what the characters in the story would say and do using each type of response.

Story starters:

• Two children are at home watching television. Each one wants to watch a different program.

• Stephanie promised to return an umbrella she borrowed from Carla several weeks ago, but forgets to bring it to school. Carla is upset because the umbrella belongs to her mother who expects it back today.

• Manny and Vic share a room. Vic keeps his things picked up, but Manny is careless. Their father says neither one can watch television until the room is clean. Manny figures Vic has to help him clean up his half, but Vic doesn't think it's fair.

It's the first day of school and Lucy wants a desk next to her friend Katrin, but all the desks around Katrin are filled. She asks Richard to move, but Richard likes where he's sitting.

Lead a follow-up discussion.

Discussion Questions:

1. What happens inside us when we bury our feelings—when we deny them?
2. What can happen when we lose control of our feelings and lash out at others?
3. What kinds of things would you do and say if you wanted to use problem solving?
4. Who "wins" a conflict when people use denial? ...when they use confrontation? ...when they use problem solving? Why?

Variation:

Have older students choose one story starter and write the three endings. Allow them to work in pairs.

Conflict Resolution Strategies
Presentation and
Comprehension Check

Objectives:

The students will:

—explain strategies for handling conflicts in their own words.

—identify the conflict strategies used in stories.

—create stories as demonstrations of strategies.

Materials:

copies of the nine conflict strategies (one set per student) , or a chart outlining the strategies displayed in full view of the students

Procedure:

Introduce the activity by inviting the students to think about a time when they were involved in a conflict or observed a conflict. Suggest that they think about the events leading up to the conflict and the feelings of the people involved in the conflict.

Have the students choose partners and tell each other their conflict stories. After the pairs have shared, invite a few volunteers to retell their experiences to the entire group.

Explain that certain behaviors can help people to handle disagreements more positively and to resolve their conflicts. These behaviors are called *strategies*.

Have the students get back together with their partners. If you have made copies of the individual strategy sheets, distribute copies of the first one (Listen carefully to the other person). Otherwise, refer the students

to the chart. Present and explain the first conflict resolution strategy and give an example of a situation in which it might be used. Then direct one student in each pair to restate the strategy to his/her partner, and the partner to summarize what it means. Examine each of the remaining strategies in the same manner:

• Explain your position without blaming the other person.
• Allow time to cool off.
• Problem solve together to create a "win-win" situation.
• Be willing to compromise.
• Say you're sorry.
• Use humor.
• Ask for help.
• Know when to walk away.

After all of the strategies have been presented and explained, check for comprehension. Read the following nine scenarios and, after each one, ask the students to identify the strategy used. If the students have copies of the strategy pages, ask them to hold up the page that shows the strategy used in that scenario. If the chart is used, ask a volunteer to point to the strategy used. The other students can use "thumbs up" or "thumbs down" to show agreement or disagreement.

Conflict Resolution Scenarios

• Cherisse waited half an hour after school for her friend Jonelle, who had promised to walk home with her. Cherisse and Jonelle had made the arrangement at lunch time. After waiting 30 minutes, Cherisse went to Jonelle's classroom and asked the teacher if Jonelle had left yet. The teacher said that Jonelle had run out of the room as soon as class was dismissed. When Cherisse saw Jonelle walking towards her the next morning, she was so angry and hurt that she ignored her. Jonelle ran after her, saying, "Let me explain, please!" Finally Cherisse thought that maybe she should listen to what Cherisse had to say. Maybe she had a good reason for leaving school suddenly. Sure enough, Jonelle explained that, just before the end of school, she remembered that her mom had told her to get home fast for an appointment with the dentist. She further explained that her mom threatened to ground her if she came home late. Cherisse was glad that she listened to Jonelle carefully instead of losing a friendship over hurt feelings. (*Listen carefully to the other person.*)

• Marco and his cousin Lidia lived close to each other and they shared a bike. They agreed to use the bike alternately, Marco one week, Lidia the next. One week Lidia forgot to return the bike to Marco and she went riding off to a friend's house. Marco was counting on using the bike to ride to soccer practice and couldn't find Lidia or the bike. He was very upset. When Lidia returned home on the bike, Marco started screaming at her and grabbed the bike away from her. Lidia remembered two occasions when Marco forgot to return the bike to her so she started yelling back. They were both losing their tempers. Finally Lidia said, "Take the bike. We can talk this over after we've had time to cool off. How about tomorrow after school?" (*Allow time to cool off.*)

• Arjel thought that his classmate Kenny was to blame for the class losing 10 minutes of free time. Kenny was talking to someone in his group about the homework after the teacher told the class to be quiet. Others were talking and giggling, too, but Arjel only saw Kenny talking. After school, Arjel stomped out of class grumbling to himself. When Kenny asked why he was so mad, Arjel wanted to put the blame on him for the loss of free time, but he replied instead, "I'm really mad that we missed our free time. I was working on a picture for the art fair and wanted to finish it today. I'm upset that everyone couldn't get quiet when the teacher asked us to." (*Explain your position without blaming the other person.*)

• When Jessica struck out at bat in the bottom of the ninth inning , she felt terrible. Her friend and classmate, Nina, made it worse by blaming her for the team's loss. "We could have won, Jess," shrilled Nina. "Why didn't you try a little harder to hit the ball? Geez, now we're out of the playoffs!" Jessica wanted to cry, but she knew that the team's loss wasn't her fault alone. She took a deep breath and said, "I'm really sorry that we lost the game, Nina. I feel bad, and I know you do, too. That pitcher was sure awesome." (*Say you're sorry.*)

• When Kyle accidentally tripped over Andy's foot walking into the assembly, he didn't have a chance to apologize because his teacher was hurrying the class to their seats. He felt nervous because he knew Andy was short-tempered. On the way back to class, Andy went up to Kyle, pushed him and accused Kyle of kicking him deliberately. When Kyle tried to explain, Andy pushed him again. Kyle said firmly, "Hey, I'm not interested in fighting," and headed for the classroom before Andy could hurt him. (*Know when to walk away.*)

• The two groups of boys faced each other on the basketball court. It was lunch recess and both groups wanted to use the full court for a game.

"We have a problem here," said Darcy, "Can't we work something out?"

"O.K., you play half court with your teams and we'll play the other half," replied Mai Lei.

Jimmy chimed in, "That's not as fun as playing full court. Why don't you guys use the whole court for ten minutes; then we can play on it for the remaining ten."

"I have another idea," said Darcy. "We can play each other using the full court and rotate players in and out every time a basket is made. That way we all get a chance to play full court."

"Sounds like an idea," answered Jimmy. "What do you think, guys?" (*Problem solve together to create a "win-win" situation.*)

• Mr. Cruz was returning homework and test papers. Mindy glanced at the paper that was passed back to her. Thinking that it was her homework, she began tearing it up. When Ahmed looked over her shoulder and saw that it was his math test, he shouted, "Hey, what are you doing with my test? My dad wants to see all of my test grades!" Surprised and embarrassed, Mindy stared at the shredded paper and put her hands to her reddened face.

"Oh...," she giggled, "I knew that. I thought your dad liked putting together jigsaw puzzles."
(*Using humor if the situation calls for it.*)

• Brad and his sister Farah were playing ping pong at the recreation center on Saturday afternoon. They were using the paddles that they checked out from the equipment room. Two girls came into the room and started looking around for something. "Wait a minute, here they are," exclaimed one of the girls. "Those two are using them."

"Hey, give us back the ping-pong paddles," the other one said to Farah and Brad, "I left them on this table two days ago."

Brad answered defensively, "They can't be yours. We checked them out of the equipment room just a few minutes ago."

"I don't care where you got them," replied the girl, "They're mine and I want them back."

"Hold on," said Farah, we'd better go to the recreation leader and ask her to help with this problem.

"Fine by me," answered the girl.
(*Ask for help when you need it.*)

• Ben and his brother Adam promised not to argue or fight if Mom took them for a day hike in the mountains.   Both were excited about spotting birds and recording them so they could earn their nature badges in scouts. Mom had only one pair of binoculars and warned the boys that they would have to share them on the hike. Adam talked to Ben before the hike, "Look, man, I really need to record more birds than you. Let me hold the binoculars, and after I see a bird on my list, I'll pass the glasses on to you."

"Wait a minute," answered Ben calmly. "It wasn't my fault that you lost your last check list. I think that we should compromise. You carry the glasses for half an hour; then I'll get them for half an hour. The person holding the glasses will get to see a bird first before passing them to the other person. That way, whoever holds the binoculars knows he'll see the bird before it flies away."

"All right," shrugged Adam. "I guess that's only fair. Then we won't argue and get Mom upset." (*Be willing to compromise.*)

When the students have shown that they understand and can identify all nine strategies, invite them to create new scenarios to represent each one. Either assign one strategy to each pair of students or ask the students to form small groups and create stories for two or more of the strategies. Have the students read or perform their scenario(s) and ask the other students to identify the strategies used. Conclude the activity by facilitating further discussion about the strategies.

Discussion Questions:

1. Which of the strategies do you find easiest to use and why? Which are hardest for you?
2. Why is it better to choose a strategy to deal with a conflict, rather than just react automatically?
3. What will help you remember these strategies when you are in the middle of a conflict?

1. Listen carefully to the other person.

Let the other person explain his or her side of the story. Pay close attention and try to understand the person's feelings and point of view.

2. Explain your position without blaming the other person.

Tell your side of the story and express your feelings in a non-threatening way. Use I-statements such as "I feel angry" or "I'm upset" instead of saying, "You made me mad." Using I-statements makes it easier for the other person to listen to you.

3. Allow time to cool off.

If either of you is extremely angry, tired, or "out-of-control," it may be better to agree on a later time to deal with the problem. Allowing a cooling off time for one or both of you may prevent a bigger conflict.

Hey Rodney, why don't we work together on this instead of getting frustrated with each other? You have some great ideas here, but I see some mistakes in spelling and grammar. I could help you with them; and I could use some of your ideas.

Maybe you're right. We could practice in front of each other, too. This way we'll get a better grade on our group presentation.

4. Problem solve together to create a win-win situation.

Make it your goal to find a resolution that both of you can accept. This is best done when both of you are calm enough to consider each other's point of view. You may need to try one or more other strategies first, such as apologizing or listening carefully to the other person's side of the story. Problem solving may also lead to compromise.

5. Be willing to compromise.

Both persons in a conflict must cooperate in order to reach a compromise. You will probably have to *give up* something, but you will *get* something, too. Use problem solving to reach a compromise both of you can agree on.

6. Say you're sorry.

If you're responsible for the conflict, say, "I'm sorry, I didn't mean to do it," or "I'm sorry we got into this fight."

Saying, "I'm sorry," doesn't necessarily mean that you admit any wrongdoing. "I'm sorry" can just be a way of saying, "I know that you are hurt and angry and I feel bad about that."

A problem often gets worse when one person feels badly and thinks the other person doesn't care — or care enough. This feeling can be eased by a simple "I'm sorry."

7. Use humor if the situation calls for it.

Making light of a conflict, without making fun of the other person, may ease the tension both of you feel. Humor generally works best when you direct it toward yourself in a natural, lighthearted way. This may help the other person realize that the situation isn't as bad as it seems.

Excuse me, Miss Pratt. We're having a disagreement over here and can't seem to work it out. Can you help us?

8. Ask for help when you need it.

When no one can suggest a solution, it's best to ask someone else to step in and help resolve the conflict. The new person can bring new ideas and a fresh perspective to the problem.

9. Know when to walk a way from a conflict.

If you find yourself in a situation where you might be physically hurt, walk or run away. If you think the other poerson might become violent, it's best to say you're sorry and leave quickly rather than try to save face or be tough.

I Got Into a Fight Because I Was Already Feeling Bad
A Sharing Circle

Objectives:

The students will:

—explain how feelings from one situation are transferred to other situations.

—identify strategies for avoiding conflicts that result from a residue of bad feelings.

Introduce the Topic:

Our topic today is, "I Got Into a Fight Because I Was Already Feeling Bad." This topic is about a type of experience that is very common. Have you ever been in a bad mood — feeling sad, worried, angry, or even sick — and gotten into an argument or physical fight with someone as a result? Maybe your bad feelings were because of something that happened at home or school and you lost your temper with someone who was completely uninvolved. Tell us why you were feeling bad and how the fight started. The topic is, I Got Into a Fight Because I Was Already Feeling Bad."

Discussion Questions:

1. How did you look and act when you were feeling bad? How do you think you came across to others?
2. How did the other person react when the problem started?
3. How can we avoid carrying negative feelings from one situation to other situations?

A Time I Was Afraid to Face a Conflict
A Sharing Circle

Objectives:

The students will:
—describe conflicts that they tried to avoid.
—explore their fears about conflict.

Introduce the Topic:

Conflict is normal and happens all the time, but usually it's not at all pleasant. Sometimes just the thought of getting into an argument or fight is scary. Today we're going to talk about times when our fear of conflict got the best of us. The topic is, "A Time I Was Afraid to Face a Conflict."

See if you can remember a time when you went out of your way to avoid a conflict. Maybe you broke or lost something that belonged to a member of your family, and you stayed out as late as possible so you wouldn't have to face them. Or maybe you received a bad grade in school and deliberately "lost" the test paper or report card because you knew that your parent would get mad and threaten to ground you. Has anyone ever challenged you to a fist fight, which you dreaded and tried to avoid? Have you ever walked a block or two out of your way in order to stay clear of the neighborhood bully or some gang members? Tell us what happened and how you felt about yourself for being frightened. Take a few moments to think about it. The topic is, "A Time I Was Afraid to Face a Conflict."

Discussion Questions:

1. Why do we dread conflicts and try to avoid them?
2. Were you able to avoid your conflict forever, or did you finally have to face it? If you had to face it, was it as bad as you imagined it would be?
3. Do you think being very skillful at handling conflicts would make facing them easier? Why or why not?

Additional Sharing Circle Topics

I Got Blamed for Something I Didn't Do
How Conflict Makes Me Feel
A Time When Sharing Prevented a Fight
How I Helped a Friend Resolve a Conflict
I Got Into a Conflict
Something That Really Bothers Me
I Observed a Conflict
A Time When I Was Involved in a Misunderstanding
I Was Angry at One Person, But Took It Out on Someone Else
A Time Someone Put Me Down But I Handled It Well
I Accidentally Made Somebody Mad
I Started a Conflict Between My Friends
A Time Humor Saved the Day
We Resolved a Conflict By Ourselves
A Time I Listened Well to Someone I Disagreed With

Jalmar Press and Innerchoice Publishing are happy to announce

a collaborative effort under which all Innerchoice titles will now be distributed

only through Jalmar Press.

To request the latest catalog of our joint resources for use by teachers, counselors

and other care-givers to empower children to develop inner-directed living and

learning skills

call us at: (800) 662-9662

or fax us at: (310) 816-3092

or send us a card at: P.O. Box 1185, Torrance, CA 90505

We're eager to serve you and the students you work with.

By the way, Jalmar Press / Innerchoice Publishing have a new series coming up
that can give you all the necessary tools to teach emotional intelligence to all your
students, grades K - 12.

Three titles will be available in fall, 1998.
Write or call for the latest information or to place your order.